Composing
Public Space

Composing Public Space

Teaching Writing in the Face of Private Interests

Michelle Comstock • Mary Ann Cain • Lil Brannon

AFTERWORD BY **NANCY WELCH**

BOYNTON/COOK
Heinemann
Portsmouth, NH

Boynton/Cook Publishers, Inc.
361 Hanover Street
Portsmouth, NH 03801–3912
www.boyntoncook.com

Offices and agents throughout the world

The authors and publisher wish to thank those who have generously given permission to reprint borrowed material:

"Fire" from *The Sea Accepts All Rivers & Other Poems* by Judy Sorum Brown. Copyright © 2000 by Judy Sorum Brown. Reprinted by permission of the author.

Library of Congress Cataloging-in-Publication Data
Comstock, Michelle.
   Composing public space : teaching writing in the face of private interests / Michelle Comstock, Mary Ann Cain, and Lil Brannon.
      p. cm.
   Includes bibliographical references.
   ISBN-13: 978-0-86709-598-2
   ISBN-10: 0-86709-598-9
   1. English language—Rhetoric—Study and teaching—United States.
2. College teaching—Political aspects—United States. 3. Academic freedom—United States. 4. Privatization in education—United States. I. Cain, Mary Ann. II. Brannon, Lil. III. Title.

PE1405.U6C662 2010
808'.042071—dc22   2010016360

Editor: Charles I. Schuster
Production: Lynne Costa
Cover design: Night & Day Design
Cover photograph: Terry Schmitt
Typesetter: Drawing Board Studios / Valerie Levy
Manufacturing: Valerie Cooper

Printed in the United States of America on acid-free paper
14   13   12   11   10   VP   1   2   3   4   5

CONTENTS

ACKNOWLEDGMENTS

In this book we attempt to create space—breathing space, public space, space of limitlessness and restriction, possibility and emptiness. In writing this book, our hope was to create an opening space on the process of doing academic work, a public space for showing the process of thinking together while calling into question the seamless spaces that academic work traditionally constructs. Yet even while we perform our work in these pages, we are always leaving things out—often the most important things: those conversations and visions that our friends and colleagues shared with us during the five years of its construction. We owe all of them thanks. We owe particular thanks to the many teachers of writing who read various chapters in various drafts—The UNC Charlotte Writing Project Teacher Consultants, particularly, Cindy Urbanski, Jennifer Pooler, and Tony Iannone; the UCD English Department faculty, particularly Gillian Silverman, Rick VanDeWeghe, and Nancy Linh Karls; the IPFW Rhetoric and Composition Reading group, including Steve Amidon, Stuart Blythe, Avon Crismore, Deb Huffman, George Kalamaras, Suzy Rumsey, and Sara Webb-Sunderhaus; colleagues who believed in us—Nancy Welch, Cindy Onore, Tony Scott, John Bradley, Phil Woods, and Troy Bigelow; and the writers who reminded us of the importance of the project. We are particularly indebted to Chuck Schuster who listened to our words and helped us find a way to make them public. To Cy and Susan Knoblauch and George Kalamaras who kept the home-fires burning, leaving spaces for composing. And to supportive friends and family—Don and Ruth Comstock, Martha Jane Brazy, and the Summers family, who cheered us on from that first inkling of a draft in 2003. We want all of you to know that though we are out of space, that the open space you created, this public space, is written with and through your participation in our lives.

1 | **Breathing Space**

Against the Privatization of Classrooms

What makes a fire burn
is space between the logs,
a breathing space. . . .

So building fires
requires attention
to the spaces in between,
as much as to the wood.

When we are able to build
open spaces
in the same way
we have learned
to pile on the logs,
then we can come to see how
it is fuel, and absence of the fuel
together, that makes fire possible.

—Judy Brown, "Fire"

Picture this: One morning you wake up to your clock radio, as usual. What is unusual is that the sound you are hearing is not a song or even the announcer's voice, but your own voice, your voice from the classroom. A fifteen-second sound bite from a fifty-minute class you taught the week before has made its way first to local talk radio, and now, as you listen, to the national news summary on one of six local Clear Channel stations, a mega conglomerate radio corporation. The words used to describe your voice are "rants," "lies," and "political." Even before you get out of bed, the phone begins to ring and ring and ring. No matter that you have a full day of teaching ahead. The media firestorm has begun.

Scenes from your teaching race fast-forward in your mind as you rise to face the expected barrage of questions. You review how you tell students that sharing their knowledge, opinions, information, and experiences is a requirement; writing is an important means by which they will do this. You recall modeling how to show respect by engaging all viewpoints and at the same time showing how you have developed your own. You stress, in class and on the syllabus, that respect and tolerance for differences are paramount; students must feel comfortable expressing their points of view. You can't imagine why your voice, your classroom, is on the airwaves and is being represented in this way. You naively thought that the conversations and debates in your classroom were safe from such maelstroms of public scrutiny, censure, and rage.

So thought Jay Bennish, a tenth-grade social studies teacher at Overland High School in Aurora, Colorado, who woke up to his own voice on the radio. One of his students, Sean Allen, in Bennish's class for barely a month, had secretly recorded twenty-one minutes and forty seconds of his teacher's fifty-minute Accelerated World Geography lecture from February 1 on his MP3 player.[1] Sean brought the recording to his father, Jeff, seeking to convince him that Bennish was "trashing Bush" and indoctrinating students with his personal viewpoints about the United States, even going so far as to compare George W. Bush's use of language to Hitler's. Sean later told reporters that he was tired of hearing Bennish's "one-sided" viewpoints. "I've been [in] his class four weeks," said Sean Allen, "and I've never heard another side" (CBS/AP 2006, par. 11).

After four weeks of complaining to his skeptical father about the "liberal" viewpoints being imposed upon students by Bennish, Sean had decided to take matters into his own hands. He recorded just enough of Bennish's February 1 lecture to prove to his father that Bennish was offering his own political opinions instead of just factual subject matter about geography.

Before speaking to the principal (or anyone else from the Cherry Creek School District), the senior Allen first sent a message to *Washington Times* columnist and weblogger Walter Williams. Williams promptly ran a blog on February 22, "Indoctrination of Our Youth," denouncing Bennish for brainwashing his students and not teaching geography, and calling for teachers in public schools and universities to be prohibited from "academic dishonesty" and "proselytizing" to students (Williams 2006, par. 12). Then, after Jeff Allen contacted Williams, the school district received an out-of-state email about Williams' editorial, and Bennish himself received an email from Williams. That same day, Allen filed a complaint with the school principal, which was forwarded to the Cherry Creek school district, and threatened to make the tape "public." Jeff Allen then took the further step of vetting Sean's tape with local talk show host, KOA's Mike Rosen, who broadcast a show on the material on March 1 and also offered Sean's twenty-one-minute recording as a podcast online. (KOA had been offering a "bounty" for recordings of "radical teachers" like Ward Churchill.)

In going to KOA, Jeff Allen made sure that he was not the only one who believed Jay Bennish's perspective should not matter. He also recruited those in positions to keep it from mattering to act upon this belief, setting into motion a chain of events that, once begun, took on a momentum far greater than any individual could control. First, Rosen denounced Bennish on the basis of Sean Allen's recording of less than half of Bennish's February 1 class. Shortly thereafter, KOA's newspaper affiliate, *The Rocky Mountain News*, published an editorial that similarly denounced Bennish for presenting "fringe" viewpoints in the classroom (Carroll 2006, 38A). The media frenzy kicked into full gear with the aggravated corporate rivalry between Fox News, who interviewed the Allens on *Hannity and Colmes* (Sean Hannity affectionately dubbing the younger Allen "junior") and NBC/MSNBC, whose Matt Lauer interviewed Bennish on the *Today Show* (Mullen 2006).[2] On the Web, the commentators had already kicked into gear with blogs by conservative commentators Williams and Michelle Malkin, among others.

For teachers of writing, what happened to Bennish could easily happen to them. College writing teachers often censor themselves or take a "neutral" classroom position so as not to "offend" their students. Some like Elizabeth Ito lost their positions because they dared to oppose the war with Iraq. Later in this book we will explore Bennish's and other stories to show just how threatened are the public spaces of our classrooms. But for now we want you to think with us about why this matters.

Representations of Public Space

Jay Bennish tried to treat his classroom as public space, the kind we believe is vital to classrooms at all levels of instruction. You may ask, What kind of "public" spaces are we advocating and how are they different than the public spaces that corporate media, the same corporate media that took Jay Bennish to task for being "biased," often represents as uncontrolled and chaotic? In *The Right to the City: Social Justice and the Fight for Public Space,* Don Mitchell discusses how public space often makes people fearful—such as how they might fear having to get up in front of a large number of people and present their views. He says, "Public space engenders fears, fears that derive from the sense of public space as uncontrolled space, as a space in which civilization is exceptionally fragile" (2003, 13). He draws a distinction between the desire to control public spaces and the need to claim public space as our own. This distinction is important to our book. What is happening in America today is that public space is being taken away by the wealthy elite. In Charlotte, North Carolina, for example, where Lil lives, the city of Charlotte built a new arena with public money for the Charlotte Bobcats, the professional basketball team. Private citizens must pay huge sums of money to attend events at this arena even though their tax dollars supported its construction. Mitchell finds this movement toward the closing of public space problematic while welcoming the claiming of space by everyday people (35). An example here might be where in a large meeting of seventy-five women and five men, the women—standing in a long line to use the restroom—decide after the last man exited the men's room to take over the "men's" public restroom and claim it for women. Representation, Mitchell argues, is key to public space: "The very act of representing one's group (or to some extent one's self) to a larger public creates a space for representation. Representation both demands space and creates space" (35). In the instance of Jay Bennish, one might be wondering, wasn't his classroom taken to the public airwaves? Wasn't his "private" classroom made public? In a moment we will be taking up the issue of public/private, how in common parlance we think of the airwaves as public because we all have radio access, and the classroom as "private" because only the students and teachers have access to it. Our point, however, is something very different.

The public classroom is a place where ideas can be engaged, interrogated, argued for, and investigated without fear of reprisal and in the spirit of inquiry. The public classroom allows for every idea to be questioned and critiqued, even the teacher's. What happened to Bennish was that his classroom was taken up by commercial talk radio and represented as an example of liberalism in the classroom, a representation that did not allow the students and their teacher opportunity to represent their classroom for themselves. Corporate representations of teaching and learning, we will argue, shrink public space. As writing teachers we have all experienced the commercialization of our field through the textbook and testing industry, which limit what is possible to teach and to read. The persistence of the "modes" of writing, even in the face of thirty years of research to the contrary, shows the durability of outmoded ideas when they are codified in textbooks. Our concern in this book is to show how the writing classroom can and should create public space for teachers and students to engage ideas without the restrictions of private, commercial interests.

Public Space up Close: Why It Matters to Teachers of Writing

What difference does it make to writers and teachers of writing to be able speak for themselves and, in doing so, to participate in the creation of, while at the same time claiming, public space? Why do our identities as writers and teachers matter, especially in a postmodern world that increasingly represents "identity" as fractured and unstable, or as easily obtained and just as easily relinquished? What exactly is gained in the teaching and learning of writing by the ability to speak for oneself in a public space?

Without adequate representation of their expertise in the decision-making processes of schooling, the public spaces available for teachers and students to speak will continue to shrink until the remaining public spaces become indistinguishable from the private interests that seek to dominate and control public space. Thus, this book is dedicated to creating public spaces—how to do that as writers and teachers of writing who are also scholar-teachers. The available spaces for representing who we are and what we do, we believe, are constrained in ways that make it difficult for teachers and students to re-present their identities, and thus their fullest range of perspectives, and bring these to bear purposefully and actively in their writing.

Consider, for example, the experience of "Jason," a full-time community college instructor teaching a poetry writing class.[3] During one class period, Jason led a discussion about a student poem that describes the pleasures of "recreational" drug use. This poem, written by a relatively young (twenty-something) student, sparked great debate and argument, particularly between the relatively older (forty-something) students who were openly critical of the poem's positive viewpoints about drugs, and those younger students for whom drug laws were questionable forms of social control and for whom taking drugs was an expression of individual liberty. A well-published poet himself, Jason was anxious to steer the discussion to the question of whether and how the poem functioned as a poem. At the same time, he worried that news of this debate would reach the ears of his department chair, school administrators, or, worse yet, the chatter of radio talk show hosts eager to expose the liberal biases and moral turpitude of college and university faculty. The discussion eventually took on a life of its own, which Jason embraced as important (where else would these students have the public space to speak so directly to issues that shape their lives?) and at the same time feared (for being perceived as too "liberal" and not stopping it altogether).

While full-time faculty at Jason's college are unionized (and thus cannot be dismissed without due process), tenure is not offered there; instead contracts are renewed every few years based on performance. Jason, along with countless other college and university teachers who are hired on renewable contracts, understood that student evaluations, complaints, and negative perceptions of his teaching from outside sources play a large role in whether he would continue teaching at his college. He also knew of writing teachers at other schools where poor student evaluations, even from just one semester, could be grounds for dismissal. Despite the strong engagement students had in the discussion, Jason could not finally predict how it might affect their overall evaluation of the course and, in turn, future evaluations of him for contract renewal.

Clearly Jason was in no position to speak as an "expert" on drug use, laws, and moral/ethical positions about either. And yet his expertise as a poet and a teacher of writing helped students create and then claim the public space they required to represent a range of viewpoints on the issue. But because of pressures, real or imagined, that Jason felt restricted *his* ability to join his students in this public discussion, Jason felt constrained to focus the discussion away from the more controversial topic initiated by students and toward one focused on the "neutral" aspects of poetic form. Instead of inquiring into how poetry and poetic form could deepen and even transform students' understanding of the controversy—of how poetry, as a form, could contain more than "either/or" positions, more than one-dimensional representations of self and experience, and thus bring students into contact with the complexities and contradictions of a given poet's experiences—Jason felt compelled to avoid controversy, at the expense of how he represented poetry to the students. Instead of a living, breathing poetry, Jason sought the "neutral" space of poetic form disconnected from experience. His own experiences and viewpoints became too dangerous to share and thus remained private. Public space, which presupposes a multiplicity of perspectives, in Jason's classroom contracted into reified blocs, received knowledge, and static forms.

What is lost, then, when public space contracts and private interests control it, are the living, breathing relationships that make individuals find and seek connection with and through differences, and find and seek differences with and through connection. What is lost is truth. What is lost is learning in its best and richest forms.

Privatization and the Writing Classroom

Just as Mitchell points out that we often encounter representations of public space in negative terms, we also encounter representations of private space as largely positive, a safe haven away from the uncontrolled chaos of public life. Images of privately owned land, housing, schools, even social services, are redolent with narratives of peace, prosperity, and order. Private space, as this story goes, is an oasis in the otherwise unstable public world. To maintain order and privacy, only certain viewpoints may be expressed. But perhaps more important, the means of expression further privatizes what is expressed. Only those who understand the forms, genres, methods, and conventions of these expressions can understand that a viewpoint, a self-representation, is even being expressed. To the uninitiated, such forms of expression would seem to have legitimate claims to objectivity and neutrality. It is as if no one is actually speaking; instead, the perspective is disembodied, without situation or context, as if to keep it as far removed from the messier, subjective public perspectives.

To counter this tendency, critic Edward Soja argues for an embodied understanding of historical, social, and spatial relations in a given situation, a concept he calls "spatialization." In Soja's view, spatialization simultaneously deconstructs (dismantles) assumptions about subjective versus objective accounts of reality and allows for the creation of "open" spaces of inquiry that put into question the epistemology of binary oppositions such as margin and center, open and closed, private and public. "Space," he argues, "is simultaneously objective and subjective, material and metaphorical, a medium and outcome of social life; actively both an immediate milieu and an originating presupposition, empirical and theorizable, instrumental, strategic, essential" (1996, 45). As a result, spatialization resists the closure of traditional philosophical strategies of thesis-antithesis-synthesis while allowing for the possibility of creating public spaces for improvising new individual and collective self-representations and actions, however conditional—a process Soja calls "thirdspace." For Soja thirdspace is an invitation, not a dogma, to "enter a space of extraordinary openness, a place of critical exchange where the geographical imagination can be expanded to encompass a multiplicity of perspectives that have heretofore been considered by the epistemological referees to be incompatible, uncombinable. It is a space where issues of race, class, and gender can be addressed simultaneously without privileging one over the other; where one can be Marxist and post-Marxist, materialist and idealist, structuralist and humanist, disciplined and transdisciplinary at the same time" (1996, 5). In later chapters we show how teachers and students can use thirdspace as a conceptual and practical tool for creating public spaces inside and outside the classroom. Right now, we return to the reasons why public space matters so much to us as teachers within our current economic and political context.

Most of us are familiar with privatization as an economic term. It often refers to the social and political privatization that has accompanied and promoted neoliberal[4] economic privatization over the past thirty years. Indian author Arundhati Roy gets at this best and most succinctly in her book, *Power Politics*, with regards to Enron, the Clinton administration, and the move to privatize electricity in India: Neoliberal privatization is about privatizing public resources, services, and geographic spaces. However, with regards to teachers of writing, privatization is also about privatizing expertise and decision making so that the people who are most impacted by such policies are permitted no place and no authority to speak on their own behalf—in other words, to self-represent. Teachers, as a result, are constrained by school administrations and school boards, unable to speak as citizens within and beyond their classrooms,[5] despite the fact that students are still allowed to do so. Consequently students are expected to construct positions and viewpoints with no examples to follow, and with little or no intervention or challenge from the writing teacher, who, in most matters of public concern, is not considered an "expert." Instead, what writing teachers are most typically considered "experts" in are the objective "skills" of grammar, mechanics, and forms of writing such as argumentation. By narrowly defining teacher's expertise in this way, writing teachers are further restricted from claiming and making public space in the classroom.

While creating public space emphasizes the need to make room for many and diverse voices to be heard and engaged, and for all participants to explore the contradictions, coherences, and conflicts of their various identities in relation to each others', privatization instead requires that some voices remain "private" and that some identities stay in the shadows, and overall characterizes public space as too "dangerous" for "impressionable" students of any age. Of course, there is a difference to be drawn between the privatized spaces of what ought to be public concern and the private life of a citizen. Nancy Welch draws this distinction in her discussion of abortion rights. The public debate about abortion has become privatized, she claims, when doctors and teaching hospitals decide to eliminate curricula about abortion procedures (2008). However, one's right to privately determine whether to bear a child is the kind of legitimate private space that public debate has enabled. Ironically, politically charged topics such as abortion are often restricted from the writing classroom, while individuals seeking abortions as private citizens face more and more restrictions on their access, despite the public's overwhelming support (77 percent) for the right to an abortion (Lake Research Partners 2006, 2).

Thus, when writing teachers' expertise is limited to "skills" divorced from the actual contexts and lived experiences of both teachers and students, a further privatization occurs in terms of limiting what identities can be represented within the classroom. Without collective organization and educational strategies to resist further privatization and to reclaim and/or create the public spaces essential for learning and teaching in a democracy, literacy education will, as Elspeth Stuckey has argued in *The Violence of Literacy*, continue to contribute to, rather than challenge, the social inequality and injustice that privatization fosters. As a result, the public spaces necessary for democracy will continue to shrink, in effect narrowing the breathing spaces we all require to write, teach, and live together.

In some writing classrooms the effects of privatization may be subtle. We may, for example, be inclined (or have the privilege) to ignore how our writing curriculum is tied to corporate interests and consumerist culture. We may adopt the role of neutral facilitator, offering our students a plethora of choices in readings, assignments, and rhetorical strategies. Such moves may seem to privilege a democratic classroom with its emphasis on freedom of choice. If such choices are situated as political and social (for example, showing a particular film monetarily supports and gives voice to a particular group of interests and allows the classroom to participate in the whole collective production/distribution process), and not simply "market choices" (for example, individuals choosing from a number of available isolated, neutral products), then the class could help students and teachers connect their decisions to larger institutional and political situations and thus develop more empowered, knowledgeable choices. Even so, we often settle for the role of consumer over producer and actor. Resisting privatization is not a process of sitting back and identifying and labeling "bad guy corporations"; it's about recognizing the processes of marginalization and oppression that accompany the loss of public space (the loss of the public good, of diversity, difference, and dialogue) and creating it anew. If, for example, a teacher sees her individual ability to choose a textbook as automatically empowering, without recognizing how this choice may be a poor substitute for collective inquiry and decision making regarding campus labor practices or curriculum design or without fully understanding the constraints already in place on the production of textbooks by market forces, she may be ignoring possibilities for creating public space and for creating larger institutional and social change.

Toward Collective Inquiry of the Writing Classroom

This book strives to create the space and time for collective inquiry and the making of public space, an often messy, slow process that doesn't fit into the clean, linear categories of conventional research. Feminist researchers like Sandra Harding and Nancy Tuana have long critiqued conventional research's claims to objectivity, uncovering the highly situated political nature of such research. We concur that "objectivity" is not created through cleaner methods and instruments but through collective inquiry, a dialogue among participants, where one asserts a subjectivity that is responsive to others in order to contribute to a larger understanding of a question or issue. This sort of inquiry is less conclusive and doesn't create individual heroes, only groups and processes.

Many of us teacher-researchers are under the constraints of the conventional model of research, which privileges the individual researcher and a highly compartmentalized line of inquiry. Lil and Michelle saw this struggle played out at a recent National Writing Project (NWP) spring conference. While NWP participants gathered in Washington, D.C., to lobby legislators for funding, the NWP emphasized the growing importance of teacher research not only to foster better, more informed teaching practices but also to provide a body of evidence (demonstrated outcomes) for national funding sources. Patricia Lambert Stock, award-winning literacy researcher and longtime advocate of teacher research, was the keynote speaker and used her talk to profile a particular local teacher-researcher who responded to a problem of student engagement with a mock trial assignment. Patti carefully outlined this teacher's research process—his hypothesizing, testing, and sharing results through the demonstration and feedback structures created by NWP. Lil and Michelle saw strong connections between Patti's work and our own in its emphasis on empowering teachers and honoring the work that we already do. This in itself is a radical political act.

Patti's presentation also left Lil and Michelle with several questions, which they addressed with her one-on-one after the presentation: Why did Patti use the traditional research model (that is, ask a question, do background research, construct a hypothesis, test the hypothesis by doing an experiment, analyze the data and draw a conclusion, and communicate the results) to frame the case study? Who was her audience? Isn't the research process highly contextualized within teachers' subjectivity (their various cultural, racial, economic, and class identifications) and the inquiry process they share with other teachers? Where is the space for political and social reflection on the research context and process? Although Patti was very receptive to their questions and wanted to talk at length about her approach, she needed to move on to another scheduled meeting. Her quick response was that she didn't have enough space in her book to account for the rich research context and the multilayered, multiparticipant research process. A case study of one particular teacher/researcher's research process allowed for a streamlined illustration of the traditional scientific model at work. It is a narrative that might empower individual teachers who feel isolated in their work and a story that clearly illustrates teachers' regular use of objective scientific methods in their teaching. Such a narrative can prove highly useful to teachers who seek necessary academic and political legitimacy, but Michelle and Lil left Patti's talk speculating about possible side effects. What about research models that encourage teachers to question and not simply adopt traditional methods? What about other research paradigms based on narrative inquiry or action research? What about models that create a truly democratic, public research process, a process that allows diversity and brings together seemingly incompatible viewpoints?

This is what our book sets out to represent—a collective process of inquiry that comes out of our shared identification as writing teachers (an identification that crosses institutional, higher education vs. secondary education boundaries) and draws on a diverse set of narratives and disciplines to address issues of privatization and public space in our classrooms. Our book explores how privatization has shaped core concepts in academic literacy such as professionalization, authority, and expertise. Furthermore, we speak as feminist scholars, writers, and teachers who are concerned with how privatization continues to determine who has the right to express themselves, when that expression can take place, whose voices count, and what textual and other spaces are available for public discourse to occur.

Each of us also represents different institutional contexts, from Ph.D.-granting research university (Lil) to regional "comprehensive" university serving primarily local populations (Mary Ann) to urban campus shifting to a research-centered focus (Michelle). We also represent different experiences of rank as well as generations of scholars, from full professor with over thirty years of university (including writing program administration) experience to assistant professor exploring new technologies and spaces for writing. Each of us approach the problem of privatization of writing and writing education from various disciplinary perspectives within English studies. These would include the following:

- **Rhetorical theory**: How do common sense views of "private" and "public" help create increasingly privatized notions of professional expertise, placing more and more of public discourse and debate exclusively into the hands of "qualified" professionals, while at the same time undermining such expertise in general as "elitist" and "out of touch" with the real world? How do schools, universities, and colleges depend upon such privatization for their authority and power in society and at the same time find that authority and power more and more controlled by private, corporate-controlled interests? How does privatization contribute to the fragmentation of previously coherent bodies of knowledge, as well as the human bodies through which that knowledge is collectively known and enacted?

- **Feminist theory and praxis**: How has the female body (particularly those of writing teachers, the majority of whom are women) as well as the concept of embodiment, as theorized by feminists, become privatized, and in the process, how has that body been set in opposition as a "safe," private space that contrasts with the "dangers" of public space? How does disembodiment function as a code for the male body and masculinity, placing a higher value on what common sense tells us is "neutral" and "objective" and thus more "true" within and across curricula, classroom spaces, and in physical, emotional, psychological, and spiritual embodiments of writing teachers and students? How do such oppositions serve to prevent the teaching and learning of collective practices of organization that lead to the creation and maintenance of public spaces, as was the case with mass reform movements in labor, civil rights, and peace?

- **Sites of literacy education:** What effects does privatization have on the public spaces of education, with its insistence on increasing surveillance and accountability, a "McDonaldization" of teachers as expendable, and a lack of accountability for charter schools funded by public money, as well as privatized curriculums, testing, and materials supported by corporate dollars? These public spaces include university writing and rhetoric courses, community service learning sites, activist interventions in labor and peace movements, mobile community literacy activism, and K–12 teacher training in public schools.

■ **Digital literacy and the problem of public space:** How do new technologies expand the possibilities for public participation while at the same time privatization ensures that fewer and fewer public spaces are available for audiences to know of and support such productions? How does privatization guarantee that even "community" audiences remain "private" and thus unavailable to writers/producers and to each other for comment, debate, and discussion of common interests and concerns?

These four perspectives work as separate strands that, at the same time, weave within, between, and among our individual as well as collective discussions of breathing space versus privatization. Conventional research, with its univocal narrative and discrete disciplinary structures, doesn't provide the space for the sort of collective inquiry and improvisation that our collective identities require.

Michel de Certeau offers an important aphorism that may explain what we are trying to do in our book. The aphorism is, "what the map cuts up, the story cuts across" (1984, 129). De Certeau is arguing about the complexity of movement between different domains of knowledge: the official knowledge, which is objective and abstract—the "map" (or what we write as academic discourse)—and practical knowledge— knowledge that is located in lived experience, in the body—"the story" (our digressions, stories, conversations). The transgressive movement cutting "across" official knowledge—the space between theory and practice, between what Paulo Freire calls knowledge and action—is the terrain we want to explore in this book. We want to crisscross the "map" of composition—the official discourse—with divergent "stories." This book is our attempt to work both within and against the dominant modes of knowing within the academic: empiricism and critical analysis. Though these ways of knowing are part of this project, we also offer the "other": knowledge that is subjective, grounded in our daily lives and our personal experiences. This "knowledge" is banished from academic argument and is labeled as unimportant—not serious—naïve— personal. We will include this "active body" of knowledge as part of our work to make visible the connections between our local circumstances and the global forces at work in and through us—even as we work to resist such domination.

Our guiding assumption is that students and teachers must have the power to both self-represent (to articulate their various subjectivities) *and* participate in collective inquiry and decision making (put their viewpoints and interpretations in transformative dialogue with others and in response to circumstances) in order to create a truly public space within our schools. Thus, we have chosen to use formats and structures that support the dialogic dimensions of our textual exchanges. The formats themselves guide the inquiry and vice versa. In order to preserve the sense of immediacy, spontaneity, and openness that we felt characterized our exchanges, we have had to alter and, at times, completely reinvent conventions that many readers might ordinarily expect in academic writing. For instance, all five chapters that follow take a variety of hybrid forms. Chapter 2, for example, offers threads of traditional academic arguments on privatization and its impact on writing instruction. However, these arguments are positioned within the conversations that gave rise to them. This hybrid form inverts the conventional hierarchy of central, academic text over marginal, supporting comments. Throughout the chapter, we offer meta commentary within text boxes (that is, reflections on our initial formulations as we return to them over time) that reflect our individual voices within the dialogue we have had with each other about specific points raised, about the composing processes we

MARY ANN: I've been thinking a lot about our design discussion and realized it ties in to what I'm doing with academic versus alt/dis in my graduate class this spring. I've invited (not assigned—this was an option) the students to address the theoretical readings we've done on community by writing hybrid texts—that is, I wanted them to give me their "review" of these theorists in relation to each other and to construct their own positions in relation to the theorists, and at the same time use whatever genre(s) they saw fit to do this. My theory was that drawing from both academic and other, more experientially driven genres might help them create bridges between their own and academic discourse. At the very least, it would create a discursive space from which they could speak differently than from either academic or experiential knowledges.

In our discussion of these texts, they surprise me with how forcefully they dislike academic prose—writing or reading it. The idea of building bridges is collapsing into something more challenging to academic discourse.

LIL: I think we need to be cautious in how we think about the relation between academic discourse and other discourses. I want to still claim a place for academic discourse as a powerful way of knowing—the "map" isn't necessarily "evil" but is certainly difficult. Lived experience can be just as problematic—it can be the common sense that supports dominant forces that are already in place. If we think in terms of bridges, the "academic" is supposed to give us another way of understanding the lived experience: It can be the bridge to our "knowing" our daily lives in different terms. But if that bridge is collapsing—if the academic is distant and remote and alienated from the work of our students, then my hope is that this book will reclaim the power of, and the need for, both the map and the territory.

experienced as we developed this project, and even our "private" lives and their impact on our collective practice. In fact, our goal is ultimately to question the idea of a "main" text, since our questioning of and resistance to privatization also extends to discursive hegemony of the private and public texts of our lives.

Ultimately, we want the form of our text to perform what we mean when we discuss resistance to privatization, namely that we resist being read as individual voices of professional authority and instead wish to enact the collective, multivocal, dialogic exchanges we argue that democracy needs from literate citizens. Yet, even as we write about what we intend this performance to be, we realize that we are also working within the constraints we are trying to expose. Although we are attempting to reveal the accidents of the production of academic discourse by making visible its "margins" and "excesses," our text, nonetheless, is merely a different formal design, a performance, but one that we hope will have powerful effects against conventional marginalization. Most important, our text will not only critique the problems of privatization but also provide models and methods for how scholars, teachers, and writers and their students can work toward collective action to resist privatization in its most destructive forms.

Conclusion: What Is at Stake?

Much is at stake for teachers of writing; without adequate representation of their expertise in the decision-making process, the public spaces available for their representation will continue to shrink until the "public" space, the breathing space, that remains, will be indistinguishable from the private spaces that seek to dominate and control the public domain. The chapters that follow both argue for and illustrate why and how it is possible for us to claim/create these spaces for our students and ourselves.

Endnotes

1. Sean Allen later claimed to have made the recording for study purposes. Bennish questioned Allen's excuse to a CBS reporter, asking why Allen did not record the entire class.
2. "FOX Entertainment lost the Olympics to NBC and MSNBC's Keith Olbermann has a grudge match going with Bill O'Reilly. There's no love lost between these two media conglomerates" (Therese 2006, par. 1).

3. Names and identifying details have been omitted or changed to protect the identity of individuals.

4. Below is a widely used definition from "What is 'Neo-Liberalism'?" by Elizabeth Martinez and Arnoldo García: Neo-liberalism is a set of economic policies that have become widespread during the last 25 years or so. Although the word is rarely heard in the United States, you can clearly see the effects of neo-liberalism here as the rich grow richer and the poor grow poorer. . . . Around the world, neo-liberalism has been imposed by powerful financial institutions like the International Monetary Fund (IMF), the World Bank and the Inter-American Development Bank. . . . The capitalist crisis over the last 25 years, with its shrinking profit rates, inspired the corporate elite to revive economic liberalism. That's what makes it "neo" or new (2000, pars. 1, 5, 12).

5. As of this writing, Cherry Creek School teachers, including Jay Bennish, are constrained from speaking to the press or other prospective interviewers unless first approved by the district's public relations official. This was in part a response to the overwhelming presence of reporters seeking information on Jay Bennish's teaching.

2 | Creating Public Classrooms Through Storytelling

Spaces can be real and imagined. Spaces can tell stories and unfold histories. Spaces can be interrupted, appropriated, and transformed through artistic and literary practice.
—bell hooks, "Choosing the Margin as a Space of Radical Openness" (1998)

In this chapter we explore how narratives of teaching, whether those like Jay Bennish's or stories we tell about our own classrooms, bring about social transformation, allowing for or limiting our classrooms as public space. We perform this exploration as a dialogue, one that began as an email exchange several years ago in preparation for a conference presentation. Throughout the dialogue we ask each other, What political and personal stakes do we have in our teaching narratives? What kinds of transformative identities do these narratives allow? In Chapter 1, we introduced Soja's notion of "thirdspace"—an "open" space of inquiry that puts into question the epistemology of binary oppositions such as margin and center, open and closed, private and public. "Thirding" requires us to represent ourselves in these narratives as uniquely situated and able to perceive the world from both margin and center, from our "personal" lives and our professional, academic worlds, and in the process, transform both (Soja 1996, 6). As bell hooks notes, when we choose to identify— not simply to conform to or reject—cultural norms, and not simply to reproduce identities of power, prestige, and privilege, but instead from where we stand, to and for ourselves, we begin to create a space for self-representation, a public space where it is possible for teachers of writing to identify through their differences instead of in spite of them. In the following narratives we outline the material and symbolic effects of privatization not in order to simply reject them (as if we could) nor to create their static opposites (for example, the idealized liberal public sphere) but in order to make room for innovation and improvisation beyond these polarities. By exposing the conditions of privatization, we open them up for revision.

Before we move on, however, we'd like to define what we mean by improvisation because it is so central to the arguments and design of this book. In their book, *Identity and Agency in Cultural Worlds*, Dorothy Holland, Debra Skinner, William Lachiotte, Jr., and Carole Cain explain, "Improvisations are the sort of impromptu actions that occur when our past, brought to the present as *habitus*, meets with a particular combination of circumstances and conditions for which we have no set response" (1998, 17–18). When confronted with circumstances that are unfamiliar within our everyday experiences, we improvise our responses. As teachers of writing, we see how often improvisation occurs when we and our students respond to "circumstances and conditions for which [they] have no set response"—for example, those that occur when situations in our classrooms arise that seem "out of control" or when students write drafts whose audiences we cannot imagine. We also know how unpredictable, or at worst, "set," our responses as teachers can be as we attempt to read, interpret, and assess such improvisations. More often than we wish to acknowledge, we wind up settling on one perspective—looking for how a student's essay conforms to or deviates from certain forms we assume to be "correct." Or we settle on another perspective—encouraging student writers to freewrite by way of "looking within" for their "true selves," assuming language is capable of "uncovering" otherwise suppressed identities. Such forms impose particular identities on writers, as when we require students to formulate a thesis or hypothesis, beginning from a position of knowing as opposed to not knowing, or to ignore how freewriting depends upon the use of "rules" such as syntax, diction, and other forms of grammar and mechanics. From either of these perspectives, however, identities and classrooms are assumed to be somethings that already exist and thus are not subject to human agency, that is, being created. Yet when we begin to look at the "impromptu actions" that occur within "particular combination[s] of circumstances and conditions," we begin to engage this third perspective described by Holland et al. From this perspective, improvisation in the writing classroom can be valued and encouraged "as a heuristic means to guide, authorize, legitimate, and encourage" their own and others' creation of identities and spaces (1998, 18).

It is with the following classroom narratives that we begin exploring our own classroom improvisations as well as our improvisations in writing this book. However, in telling these stories in a written text such as this, we realize that the circumstances and conditions of our storytelling are, within conventional forms and genres, subject to suppression, and thus unavailable as part of our self-representation of identities. We have chosen to address this dilemma by improvising the form of our narratives so as to better reflect their circumstances and conditions and, in turn, allow us the breathing space to further improvise the identities that are imposed upon us and from which we cannot, in any absolute or final way, escape, but which we can alter and revise. We've chosen a format that makes visible the beginnings of our ongoing dialogue that has formed the basis for this book. We've created a collective voice, "Us," to assist readers in following us behind the scenes, so to speak, when we began to create this dialogue and, in turn, the early thinking and questioning that led to this book. Our intention is to expose the false starts, dead ends, and muddied thinking that is part of the academic enterprise. In doing so, we wish to demystify and thus make public how academic arguments are constructed so that a broader range of readers may be able to join us in dialogue and action. The dialogue begins with a discussion of how to textually represent our complex process of academic argument construction.

Mary Ann: I want our readers to understand this dialogue. There is a lot at stake in their staying with us.

Lil: But reading something different like this text may make people very uncomfortable. People like the well-plotted novel, the familiar poem. This hybrid discourse might take some getting use to.

Michelle: It's not that hard to follow, once you get the hang of it.

Mary Ann: When we started this project, we, too, fell into the old trap of writing "coherent" academic discourse. There is something safe about the familiar academic voice.

Lil: Yes, people can ignore it.

Michelle: We don't want people to ignore this.

Lil: So how do we help them read this book?

Mary Ann: They need to know from the start that what is most important about academic discourse is the part that people leave out. We are not leaving out those parts. As writing teachers, even in this postprocess age of composition, we still think of writing as a process. We assign drafts and revisions to our students. But we never make the messiness of our own academic writing public. We say, "Who cares about our false starts, our conversations in hallways, our arguments with each other?" But often it is these parts of writing academic discourse that are most important. We often think of them as "too private" or "nonprofessional" or otherwise irrelevant. These are most often the most interesting moments.

Michelle: They also will need to know that, after months of writing, we realized that this book had to take a different form. We couldn't be complicit with the very forces we are arguing against. How could we write a book about public space and not represent the very public nature of academic discourse?

Lil: We are risking being silenced. We are risking not being read, simply because no one will have seen anything like this. They won't imagine that the discourses that feel most comfortable are the ones we are critiquing.

Mary Ann: In my fiction class yesterday, we had a conversation very much like this one. We were discussing fiction versus antifiction (terms I've drawn from Margot Livesey's essay, "How to Tell a True Story" [1994]). Fiction presents the world as a seamless whole that makes sense, while antifiction is about showing the limits of that fiction, what it can't contain, how it is never enough to represent the truth of our experiences.

Lil: So we want our readers to think with us about this dialogue as a form of "antifiction"—an antiacademic book, if you will, where we attempt to make visible the places where our ideas spill over and refuse to be contained, where ideas get interrupted by the routines of daily life, by our teaching and travels, by our lived lives. Here we attempt to get at the truth of our "narration sickness" (Freire 1995, 52).

Mary Ann: Our readers will need to get used to seeing these textboxes. Ones like this:

> **MARY ANN:** Now, a year and a half later, as I read Kristie Fleckenstein's book, *Embodied Literacies*, I see new complexities to my argument about the dominance of text, namely that the image, along with text, dominates cultural meaning making. Citing visual critic Nicholas Mirzoeff, Fleckenstein writes, "Our current postmodern crisis is not a product of our textuality. Rather, it is a product of our imagery" (2003, 3). Literacy is both image and word, but "[b]y failing to attend to imagery, or doing so only elliptically, we cannot adequately address how our images imprison and free us, how they hurt and heal us, and how they oppress and transform us" (4). Our images, like our bodies, our "personal" lives, our emotions, and our cultural identities, have been deemed "private" and thus cut off from their social roots and their powerful shapings of "public" meanings—the cultural stories that we live by. By maintaining images as private, placed in gated communities of meaning that are available only to those with the capital to gain access, literacy, in both word and image, depends upon violence to maintain that privacy.

Lil: Textboxes aren't so bad. People see them in nonfiction all the time. Think *Newsweek, Time.* The textbox writing is about the topic, but it offers a different slant. Ours will offer reflections and revisions on our dialogue, as well as extended examples.

Michelle: But we will reverse some of the typical academic stuff. We will offer academic arguments while we simultaneously critique or talk about composing those arguments. We won't just talk about creating public space. We'll show our readers how we do it, including the missteps and blind turns we took.

Lil: Let's begin this dialogue on classroom public space with a teaching story. Creating public space for inquiry isn't easy. In fact, teaching isn't easy. Learning about one's teaching may be even harder. I say these words to myself when I think about that day that I tried to teach Bebe Moore Campbell's piece that is often anthologized as "Envy." (It is from her autobiographical book, *Sweet Summer*.) I knew leaving class that day that I was the one who was the learner. "Envy" is a piece about her growing up in a matriarchal household with her mother and aunt and her longing for a more active father in her life. I had great plans for the story.

The excerpt I wanted my students to think about narrates two incidents where Bebe longs to have a father (a male figure) in her life. Bebe lives in a house of females and says she "could have died from overexposure to femininity." In her house, "there was no morning stubble, no long johns or Fruit of the Loom on the clotheslines, no baritone hollering for keys that were sitting on the table. There was no beer in the refrigerator, no ball game on TV, no loud cussing." Only "bosoms" and "bubble bath and Jergens came from the bathroom, scents unbroken by aftershave, macho beer breath, a good he-man funk."

How I really love that story, for its use of language and for what it did for me as a reader—making racism and white privilege plain, dramatizing the problematic nature of violence.

The class had already formed into a circle by the time I arrived. "Not bad," I thought, "how quickly the class has become a community." We are really starting to feel comfortable with one another.

"What did you make of the story?" I asked Tony as I stumbled into my desk.

"Yeah, it was good. I really like the part about 'My fath-a made me a be-u-ti-ful dollhouse!'" His voice imitated how he heard the words from Bebe's mouth.

"Let's look at that part, then. Why does she become so angry? Why does she threaten her teacher with a knife she doesn't even have?"

"What she really wants is a father," Jennifer says confidently.

"Yeah, she wants a father who really cares about her, like the kid's father next door," adds Jamie.

"Does the father next door really care about his son?" I ask, thinking to myself, "That's a stupid question. I know the answer is no."

The students in unison say, "Yes."

"Wait a minute, wait a minute." Of course my students are merely confused. I search for a clarifying question.

"Isn't the father next door beating the boy with his belt?"

"Yeah."

"So how is that caring?" I ask confidently, knowing that my point is now made.

"He cares enough to spank the boy," says Stephen.

"And that is what Bebe wants," adds Jennifer, "a father who cares enough to spank her."

I slide my desk back a bit from the circle. I decide to enlist allies. "How many of you agree with Jennifer and Stephen?" I think, surely no one else could possible think this way.

All twenty-five hands go up.

I clear my throat. "Is beating a child . . . is this form of child abuse . . . caring? Surely, you don't think so." I feel anger in my voice.

"What do you mean, child abuse?" says a student to my left. "Hey, kids need spankings," says a student to my right.

I begin to feel like Bebe in the coat closet. I want to threaten them with my pretend knife. I pull out a dagger. . . . Lecture I: This story portrays two types of violence: the violence of Bebe's words and the violence against children in her neighborhood.

Paulo Freire appears on my shoulder and whispers in my left ear: "So you think Lecture I will do the trick, do you? See Christina's eyes glazing over. That's narration sickness."

I continue with the Lecture . . .

Michelle: Lil, I want to hear more about how you made the case about both kinds of violence. I could read a lot into it—for example, that Bebe's narrative provided a disturbing glimpse into the general acceptance of violence by students in your class or that your students experience violent punishment as a form of "real" interpersonal engagement. Because I'm reading Freud right now, I see correlations between how your students articulate the need for violence in raising children and Freud's interpretation of the masochistic "a-child-is-being-beaten" fantasy. In the master-slave narrative that undergirds this fantasy, the passive voice ensures a perverse, masochistic contract by exposing only the "victim"—the child who is being beaten—and not naming the perpetrator subject (Freud 1997, 99). Narratives like "kids need spankings" reinforce this contract. Retelling the story and identifying the positions (agent, victim, or third-party voyeur), as in "The father is beating the child," "The institution is beating the student," or "The teacher is beating the student," or even "I am beating myself," goes a long way toward breaking the contract where the perpetrator subject remains unnamed. Instead of silently assuming our positions in our homes and schools, instead of creating a silent contract with the unnamed perpetrator, whether it's within our family, schools, or neighborhoods, we publicize the violent relationship and our place in it. One way privatization works is to neutralize or erase the perpetrator behind standardized testing, curricula, and school vouchers. Perhaps I'm going way off track with this?

Regardless, I'm happy you are telling this story—a teacher story of "failure"—because most traditional teaching stories create some kind of generalizable objectivity or offer a performance pedagogy where teachers might don the hat of neutral questioner or rhetorical wizard. What would happen if, in a "student-centered" classroom (a scene that ostensibly undoes the master-slave narrative of education), students were to see us and themselves as desiring and learning subjects and recognize academic practices as libidinal investments—what Lawrence Grossberg calls "the particular content of a commitment" (1992, 230)? And to move to a broader question, What if they were to recognize our own dissatisfaction with (or "failure" to achieve) the "academic personality" or "neutral questioner" and join us in an attempt to transform it?

Us: One consequence of privatization that teachers of writing must face is increasing pressure to create classroom spaces that "privatize" all signs of their agency as co-creators (along with students) of knowledge and learning. Instead, teachers are represented as "objective" (or in other words, commodified) delivery systems for the "neutral" receptacles that are students. Privatization demands that our choices, our perspectives, and our experiences be erased so as not to "bias" the more "objective" authoritative voices presented within textbooks, media, and program curricula. Such curricula emphasize forms, mechanics, and grammar as neutral "skills" and "tools" for students to acquire. Yet for a teacher to disclose the "seams" behind the smooth fiction of writing as the objective acquisition of such "skills" is to expose the very fiction of privatization itself. In other words, "skills" are not simple acquisitions resulting from disciplined (albeit often alienated) labor, a labor that presumably will lead them successfully into the marketplace, but instead are part of a struggle for representation, a struggle that teachers can help guide students into and through.

That struggle is the same as what teachers themselves face on a daily basis, namely the contradictions that define the goals of education. As David Schultz writes in "The Corporate University in American Society," the need for "critical and knowledgeable citizens capable of self-governance in a democracy" is at odds with the marketplace values of "trained, subservient workers" whose production costs are placed squarely in the laps of schools (2005). A teacher's own experiences in this struggle may be valuable in making public these otherwise privatized struggles, since many, if not all, students enter the classroom believing in the seamless fiction of a market-driven economy as an uncontestable reality. From that standpoint, there are no "seams," no underworkings, no "private" accesses. A teacher's function may be not only to expose the seams that hold that fiction together but also to speak from the perspective of one who must understand and struggle through the same contradictions, albeit from different social standpoints and positions of power. In this way, a teacher may speak not simply from the perspective of Expert but as one who struggles with the same forces, offering stories, as well as inviting students to share their own, as a first step toward building a collectively produced, uncommodified knowledge base. While privatization would insist that such knowledge is merely "subjective," and, as such, threatens to confuse or dilute a writer's objectivity, creating public space requires active participation on the part of all concerned in representing a collective viewpoint or experience. One important viewpoint to explore in the writing classroom is the experience of learning to write—what all have experienced, what writing is for, for whom, and why. In this way, teachers can make visible the otherwise invisible politics of the writing classroom as part of the "antifiction," the messy seams that hold the whole fiction of why writing is (otherwise) unquestionably a "good" thing to learn. The question of what and who one is writing for would become the basis of a collective inquiry, countering privatization's imperative to keep the politics "private," unseen, and thus unavailable for inquiry, research, and debate.

Mary Ann: This binary between "violence" (here of the action of child abuse) and "peace" (presumably enacted in words, not actions) brings to mind Shirley Brice Heath's *Ways with Words*, specifically her discussion of the difference between middle-class white townspeople's rhetorical strategies of instructing children versus those of working-class blacks in Trackton. Heath notes how townspeople often pose instructions as questions, "Should we take a bath now?" as opposed to Trackton's imperative statements, "Get your rusty butt in the tub now." I had a similar moment when working with the kids of the Three Rivers Jenbe Ensemble (TRJE).[1] Kids and adults were having pizza at a local restaurant after their Saturday morning rehearsal and prior to their evening performance. One of the service learning students who worked with TRJE had left cookies for them to share. I offered to distribute them, but Agatha, one of TRJE's staff coordinators, who I fondly call "the heartbeat" of the group, with brusque humor told me, "You'll give them too many choices." I laughed, a bit uncomfortably, since that statement bled not just into how I would distribute cookies but how I related to the kids as a TRJE teacher. She proceeded to hand out cookies without asking the kids which kind they preferred. She wisely noted, as an aside, that they would trade if they wanted a different cookie.

So Lil's discomfort with her students' embrace of corporal punishment gets me to thinking about cultural and class differences around what is "violence." I, too, flinch at the thought of this father beating his children. But then I juxtapose that to the stories I've heard from African American fathers who will smack their children, in particular, their sons, in consciously deliberate recognition of the hold of that violence in the streets, gang violence, and the overall high odds of young black men being imprisoned, shot, or addicted. To put it in my own words, it's their way of resisting a palpable social and cultural violence with physical acts meant to gain attention of boys otherwise mesmerized by the pseudo-power of street violence, sometimes encoded in popular music.

I make another leap into both conservative and liberal viewpoints regarding the "violent" resistance of oppressed groups such as the Iraqi resistance, Palestinian resisters to Israeli occupation of Gaza, and, in this country, the Black Power movement's taking up of arms to defend against white takeovers of their neighborhoods and people. Conservatives would decry the "terrorist" tactics employed by these groups. Liberal pacifists (with whom I have been largely sympathetic) would decry the use of violence and instead advocate mediation and dialogue. But when I think of the kids I've encountered, both in TRJE and in the local CAP on Violence project, a court-ordered program for nonviolence education, I see how this binary between words and actions is useful in supporting privatized interests. I see how by aligning "peace" with mediation and dialogue, and "violence" with action, that we lose understanding of history and social structures, of the material conditions that give rise to oppression and its attendant violence upon the oppressed. I can understand when a grandmother tells me that the advice given her by an elder black male to give her biracial grandson, who is on the cusp of manhood, physical smacks, makes sense to her. That strong, powerful words delivered with intensity, even anger, may be the only way to wake up kids to their lack of understanding of history and their need to know it and see themselves as part of it.

For example, one day this winter, Ketu, TRJE's artistic director and one of its founders, publicly berated some of the kids for failing to have ready their presentations for Black History month. He scolded them for failing to see how the struggles of others have given us freedoms they had lacked and urged that we had to continue that struggle for freedom, building upon and taking lessons from that past. My service learning students and I felt the lesson, too; all three wrote in their class blogs about how little history they knew and of their need to know more about such struggles.

Thus, I can understand, albeit still rather abstractly, why a father might hit his son and see it as an act of resistance to the scripted lives of young black men rather than "violence." When understood in the context of not only what is done but what is said, why, to, and for whom, I can approach this understanding, even though I admit I can't see myself at this point acting in this way.

So for this reason Lil's story raises more questions than it answers for me about how to regard the violence in this book, in the ways that students see violence versus discipline, in her own relations with students.

Us: So what do you, our readers, think about all of this talk about classrooms, Freud, privatization, and violence? We make things appear dialogical—appear as though we are in command. But actually, it isn't like that at all. We began this conversation many years ago on very shaky footing. Mary Ann started writing about a book she was reading, *The Alphabet Versus the Goddess: The Conflict Between Word and Image.* She told Lil and Michelle about it in an email telling them about the author's argument that written language has changed cultures into patriarchies, in effect challenging the binary. She said that the author does a historical survey of ancient cultures to show how literacy changed them from goddess-based to male-god-based. While she conceded the implications that goddess cultures were inherently good and peaceful as problematic, she was nonetheless interested in the perspective this work offered on their work as literacy specialists. She thought this book might help them make the case for words being powerful and that could be used instead of violence.

Here is how that conversation went.

Lil: Mary Ann and Michelle—OK, my initial reaction to Mary Ann's discussion of the book, *The Alphabet Versus the Goddess*, went even beyond her own disclaimer about the limitations of the argument. It is hard for me to buy an argument that there was an ancient time—long, long ago—where patriarchy did not rule and that all women were free and equal partners to all others. It is hard for me to buy the argument that the advent of the technology of writing changed fundamentally the structure of culture. I could see how the technologies of writing made more visible how patriarchy functions and solidified patriarchal values and domination (much in the same ways that digital technologies have done in our own times) but . . .

Did I misunderstand the book's argument?

Mary Ann: Lil, I don't think you misunderstood what I've said about the book's argument so far. I do think the book is saying that goddess cultures were not patriarchal. This book starts with the first "technology," the alphabet, and how cultures changed in particular ways when laws and scriptures came into being, namely that the goddess disappeared and people started fighting over religion. Monotheism took over. I don't think, however, that the book is assuming that all women were "free and equal partners to all others" in goddess culture. It does suggest that women may have had it better then. Well, maybe that's not very different than your point—that there is no ancient long, long ago? Yet the argument goes beyond cultural changes wrought by literacy. And now you're all going to think I've lost it for even bringing this up. But here goes: It claims that literacy has changed brain functions, so that we are left-brain dominated instead of balanced more between the two hemispheres. Left brain = patriarchy. Right brain = goddess cultures. You're probably familiar with the claims made about right versus left brain. Left brain is analytical (primarily), focused on single-pointed attention, while right brain is associative (primarily), focused on holistic perception. It's not that goddess culture had it "right" (pun not intended), but that we lost the positives of that way of being when left brains took over.

OK, just so you don't think I've totally gone off the deep end and embraced determinism, let me tell you why this argument interests me. I absolutely do not buy into any notion that there is some inherent, predetermined hard-wiring of our physical being any more than I buy into the notion that literacy is inherently "patriarchal" and thus "violent." But I do think there is a relationship between technologies of writing and the cultures they exist in. I do think that alphabets shape our consciousness, shape the ways our minds and bodies move. But I agree that how we are shaped is not inherently negative.

Yes, I'm sure it sounds like I'm dredging up old stuff. We already know the relationship between the signifier and the signified is arbitrary, right? But that just doesn't explain enough for me in terms of what happens with language outside of the printed word.

Us: Not only did we not have clear ideas when we started, we had no idea how to construct a dialogic text. We thought email might help us. But take a look at what happened there:

Mary Ann (again): I've been thinking about this project, and after talking about it to Nancy Welch a little on Friday, I thought I'd better see where we all were in the process. I'm concerned that we don't really have a clear process in mind (if we did, we'd be dialoguing more). If we ever want to get this book project finished, I think we need to figure out exactly how to approach this project. I'm wondering if we shouldn't try to riff, since that seems to take more of a back and forth like real-time conversation, and email maybe stifles that. But maybe we could spend the next week (or at the very most, two), using email to brainstorm our themes, arguments, examples, stories, evidence, and so on. After that, maybe we'll have a clearer idea on how to proceed.

Let me know what you're thinking, OK? Michelle, you said you had something written already. Why don't you show it to us to get the brainstorming going (if, in fact, that's what you two want to do)?

> **Us:** While it appeared to go nowhere, the thread on alphabetic literacy did instigate another series of exchanges on the private/public binary and the effects of privatization in the classroom.

Michelle: Okay, I've been thinking about how to contribute my own classroom story to this dialogue, and while I don't really have a complete story, I do have a metaphor. I'm trying to find a metaphor for how privatization works on student/teacher bodies, and I'm toying with the metaphor of the "perverse couple." Here are some of my initial speculations . . .

In *Creativity and Perversion*, Freud scholar Janine Chasseguet-Smirgel defines "perversions" as "a dimension of the human psyche in general, a temptation in the mind common to us all" (1984, 1). After decades of analysis, she asserts that "there is a 'perverse core' latent within each one of us that is capable of being activated under certain circumstances" (1984, 1). And according to psychoanalyst Jean Clavreul, all perverse bonds (and perversion requires a bonding of some sort) require a secret contract, which is the "heart" of the perverse love affair, an affair based not on love at all but on a "pretended linking through love" (1980, 218). The "perverse couple," includes three agents: both members of the couple, who are linked through their alleged love, and a third party (a particular person, social group, institution, and so on), who is excluded from the scene but somehow endorses or counterendorses the authenticity of a normal love relation. In the perverse breakup, it's not infidelity or suffering that is the issue; it's the telling to the third party that is the scandal. The perverse couple is torn apart when one or the other makes a public allusion to their practice. The power is in the secrecy.

I'd like to note the ways my students and/or I have occupied the position of the "normal" partner, who simply submits to the perverse practices of her partner (the institution) out of what she calls duty, pity, or "love." Clavreul claims that the so-called normal partner is more in question, for it is clear that the perverse bond is sustained only by virtue of its power to fascinate the other (1980, 218). I'd like to also note the ways we have occupied the position of the third party, in attempting to witness and make public the terms of the contract. The ethic behind my inquiry is the role of love (I know, I know—a problematic term, one that usually obfuscates rather than elucidates) and desire (versus a secret, "perverse servitude") in inaugurating writing and knowledge.

Privatization works to move public goods into the private sector. It would then seem that attention to one's own libidinal investments would do the same. However, the reverse happens. In attending to passions and desires and making those investments a subject of discussion in the classroom, in recognizing passion (and fear and compassion, and so on) as the impetus of discussion itself is to de-neutralize and de-objectify the content of the course. It also brings to the surface the cravings and compulsions at work in consumerism, along with all of their political and social effects. Naming desires can diversify the classroom in ways beyond the roles and categories sanctioned by the media, corporations, and the university. If we start talking about and exploring the politics of desire, if we move toward understanding and integrating silenced and marginalized desires, we'll be less likely to buy objects or make arguments that cover over those desires and more likely to create institutional and political space for them.

My first example of a "perverse secret contract" within a school situation is a memo circulated during the initial months of the Iraq war, when academic freedom was under scrutiny in Colorado schools and universities. Not long before President Bush declared war, one of my students, a teacher in the Denver area, received a memo from her administration, the Jefferson County School District and the Jefferson County Education Association, stating that "teachers must be judicious in expressing their political opinions to avoid politicizing the classroom or disrupting the learning environment" and must provide a "neutral atmosphere." She understood the memo as a response to the controversy over a "Not my president, not my war" button a Colorado middle school teacher wore on a field trip. At the postsecondary level, freedom of speech in the classroom was also under intense discussion as the Academic Bill of Rights (inspired by conservative David Horowitz's Students for Academic Freedom campaign) gained momentum in the Colorado legislature. Had it passed, the Academic Bill of Rights would have guaranteed students "the right to expect that their academic freedom will not be infringed by instructors who create a hostile environment toward their political or religious beliefs or who introduce controversial matter into the classroom or course work that is substantially unrelated to the subject of study." A joint resolution condemned academic practices and policies that "violate First Amendment freedoms, including mandatory 'diversity training' that attempts to force students to affirm behavior or viewpoints that violate faith or conscience of students and that limit the right of individual students or student groups to speak on political, religious, and other cultural topics, including the right to speak disapprovingly of certain sexual behaviors." While I had no difficulty including the memo and the Academic Bill of Rights in my spring 2003 curriculum, other professors and teachers in the area received negative publicity and death threats for discussing the same issues in their classrooms. The teacher who had worn the button was so shocked by the vitriolic response of parents, community members, and the press (the *Denver Post* questioned her citizenship and called for retribution) that she began wearing an American flag with the word *peace* on her lapel (Fox News 2003).

> **Us:** As much as we were intrigued with Michelle's application of Freudian concepts of "secret contract" and "perverse relationships," Lil and Mary Ann were also somewhat baffled by how they actually applied to teaching in general, and teaching writing in particular. Understanding theory is relation to practice is often a difficult, even vexing operation, one that perhaps requires dialogue to move from individual, "privatized" understanding toward more "public" material perspectives.

Lil: Michelle, I'm not sure I really understand what you mean, and I need you to say more. I thought at one point you were saying that as teachers of writing we play the role of voyeur (or peeping "Jane"), on the scandalous relationship between our students in first-year writing and the institution, the pervert that tries to seduce students into submitting.

Mary Ann: I had a somewhat different read on what Michelle was saying. At first it sounded like the teacher was the voyeur on the student's "perverse" engagement with the university. But then later Michelle said that she and her students have both occupied the position of "third party," who is the spectator to the "perverse bonding" with the university. So while this does suggest what Lil is concerned about, namely that the teacher is portrayed as a voyeur, it also suggests that students and teachers may take turns in that role in relation to the university, giving witness to each other's "perverse" relationship with the institution. While I share Lil's concern about the masking of a teacher's powerful/powerless role in this scenario, it seems to me that there might be another possibility here: students as bystanders to teachers' "perverse" relationship to the institution.

Lil: What interested me in my reading of your comments (which I may have all wrong) is the dramatization of the unequal relationship between students of writing, teachers of writing, and the institution. What bothered me was how the teacher becomes bystander. And what seemed masked was the fact that the teacher and student are the institution (they are what constitute the institution and bring it into being). If we understand institution in this way, then we can see how our "roles" can be critiqued and how the politics of "engagement" can be made visible. The problem for me of the teacher as voyeur (third party) is that we hide the teacher's role as the one both all-powerful and almost powerless in the classroom.

Am I making sense here?

Mary Ann: You're making sense, Lil, and I have some questions about what Michelle is saying by way of clarification. It's easy to see how teachers are voyeurs to students, but when are students voyeurs to teachers? Is this where memos on censorship come in, documents that enact the perverse relationship of teachers to the institution, in this case requiring teachers to limit their speech and language to suit the perverse desires of the institution? Is there some hope, then, that students can make public this perverse relationship? How would that happen?

I guess I'm still having trouble understanding the idea of a "perverse" relationship and the role of a third party. What makes it possible for a third party to not be a voyeur, as Lil says, and instead make the "libidinal investments" in the classroom subjects of discussion? Just the idea of discussing "desires" and "passions" seems rather daunting in an institutional climate that shuns anything so "personal" and "private." Maybe further definition of these terms would help?

Lil: We have to be equally careful not to reduce the power differences between teacher and students. We don't want to imply an "I'm OK—you're OK" sense of equality. At the same time, I don't want to rehash the all-powerful/powerless dichotomy, either.

Michelle: Thanks for filling in some of the gaps in my bulky metaphor. I understand that if I stick with this metaphor, I'll need to explain my terms—particularly "perversion." I hope to appropriate it from both its pathological and celebratory connotations, though I'm still not sure that is completely possible or desirable. The term may carry too much weight. I use the term "perverse" not to represent a sexual category or identity, but to suggest a structural, conditioned misdirection of energy or power toward a wrong end or purpose, such as the oppression or annihilation of an Other or the self. This stands in contrast to love, which is also a process. A definition of love, fitting for this context, is offered by philosopher Alain Badiou: "It is a production of truth. The truth of what? That the Two, and not only the One, are at work in the situation. . . . Love is an inquiry of the world from the point of view of the Two" (2006, 266, 276). Unlike the perverse secret contract, where "the Two are only a machination of the one" (Badiou 2006, 271), love is a process whose method is dialogue and whose aim is the production of both alterity and truth. I'd also like to mention here that Jean Clavreul's essay, "The Perverse Couple," was a mixed blessing. It was brought to my attention by my colleague and friend, Becky McLaughlin, and we had many a chat about it before I decided to use it to build the metaphor. I use it with a great deal of hesitancy, as Clavreul follows a highly dichotomized and homophobic view of sexuality and perversion. I'm ready to accept the argument that the metaphor is hopelessly flawed by Clavreul's own conditioning; however, I also hope that I'm using it in such a way that the metaphor provides an opening for discussion about one's conscious or unconscious relationships to the institution.

Us: At this point, none of us is too certain that Michelle's theory will hold up or whether it will prove to be part of the problem of privatization. Is this version of Freudian theory capable of explaining the social, public nature of classroom relations? Or is it all just too deeply rooted in "private" concepts of self and individual?

Because the three of us expressed so much difficulty with Michelle's use of the "perverse couple" metaphor, she considered dropping it from the manuscript in order to prevent further misunderstanding. Prompted by Lil and Mary Ann's questions, Michelle reconsidered her approach. The resulting dialogue added even more layers to the metaphor and generated more analysis on how privatizing economic forces dehumanize institutional relationships. Ultimately, we decided to take the risk and keep the metaphor, along with all our attending questions and skepticism about it.

Michelle: Based on your questions, I think I know how to make the metaphor clearer and more applicable to teaching situations. Instead of stressing the subject positions within the metaphor—the pervert, the "normal" one in perverse relation to the pervert, the third party (signer, countersigner, voyeur)—I will focus on the secret contract that is the heart of the perverse relationship. The contract could be between the institution (as the big Other) and the instructor *or* between the instructor and student *or* between the student and the institution. The third party could be an imagined public or principle or policy or an actual person occupying the position of an ethical love. What makes the relationship perverse is the secret contract, not the existence of a perverse institution. I agree with you both that the institution can be conceived as its students, its faculty and staff, its policies, its history, its administrators and legislative bodies. That's the irony of the thing. We're all susceptible (dangerously so) to submitting to the big *O* version of the institution. It's a version that demands secrecy, paranoia, and elicits painful obedience (and some pleasure, too). And it brings with it its own limited notions of power and control—the kind that accompany any collusive and abusive relationship.

The limiting perverse relation, along with the limiting big O notion of the institution, is blown apart when the secret contract is broken, when the secret gets out, when as Mary Ann says, the third party bears witness to the perverse relation (or the perverseness of the relationship). I like the idea of bearing witness—it gives more ethical agency to the position of voyeur. Let's say every time we ask our students to critique or change (to bear witness to) the university structure (such as making the censorship memo part of the writing curriculum), we are betraying our own perverse relationship to it. We are refusing our role within the narrative, as well as the narrative itself.

What then would it mean to break, make public, the prescribed gender/sexual/libidinal investments we have in the institution? What different sorts of relationships, bodies, and desires would emerge and take their place? Breaking the contract is also related to the role of writing— its publicity—inside and outside the university. It again highlights the risk of putting something in writing, the risk of pointing to the false dichotomies between actions and words, as well as the risk of pointing to those things (namely desire) that are irreducible to spoken or written language.

Us: While the metaphor of the perverse couple became richer through dialogue and explanation, Michelle still needed to provide several everyday examples of the perverse relationship in the classroom, so teachers could see themselves participating in and counteracting this dynamic. Teachers could then better use the metaphor to gauge and reinvent their relationships with the institution and their students. They could engage in what Soja calls "thirding," which asks us to perceive the world from both margin and center, from both our "personal" lives and our professional, academic worlds at the same time in order to transform them.

Michelle: I want to add two classroom profiles that I think represent the perverse relationship in more everyday situations. First, however, let me clarify that there is no such thing as a "perverse classroom"; instead, the perverse relationship, whether it's between the teacher and the institution, the teacher and the student, or the institution and the student, is reinvented within the context of the classroom. Perverse acts can take numerous forms; it's the perverse structure, the mechanism of the secret contract, which is important. The perverse act is a disavowal of the position of lack of knowledge, of the human desire and need to know and learn and love (a disavowal of the openness and vulnerability of not knowing that is necessary for learning); its secret contracts and games circumvent the open space, the unknowing, necessary for a real learning and loving process.

Now to how the perverse relationship relates to privatization. I set up a perverse relationship with the institution (in this case, the institution is a fetishist and I'm the accommodating partner) when I pass out a writing assignment rubric, a script fetishized and commodified by the institution, that stands in for the messy, indeterminate reading and writing practices that happen in a classroom. Both the institution and the teacher know full well, and yet disavow, that indeed this rubric is not *it*, that it is not the vulnerable give and take of a true learning and writing situation.

Karl Marx described the fetishization of objects as the process of imbuing objects, such as the writing rubric, with magic properties, as if the object just showed up, already made, for the consumer (in this case, the student). The problem with this is that the labor (which is a social relation—one labors for oneself and/or another) involved in creating the object is hidden. The consumer sees the object s/he wants and not the labor involved. According to Marx, this is a form of creative denial—one invests an object with value but then forgets the social process of such valuing (1976, 164). This fetishization process is more likely to occur in educational contexts where learning and teaching have already become highly specialized, concretized, and commodified and where students are understood and treated as consumers. Education and learning, for example, become progressively more objectified and commodified in a capitalist society and even more so in privatized settings where investments shift from the public good to private profit. Perversion involves fetishizing, dominating over, and/or submitting to objects, roles, and scripts. Although an object isn't always a commodity, one could say that objectifying and selling learning, including the desire to learn, is a perverse act.

In order to be a good partner to the institution, the teacher needs to be a professional and keep the secret contact, which involves joining in the fetishization process, that is, pretending that the rubric does and can stand in for learning and discounting her own desires and the social process involved in creating the rubric. What makes this relationship perverse is the secret contract, the joint disavowal of the questioning dialogue necessary for learning and communication. What also makes it perverse is the exclusion or duping of the third party who would ordinarily bear witness to the authenticity of a teaching/love relation. In this case, the third party is the students. The students may also join the teacher in the contract and pretend not to know what's really going on. The teacher has the ability to expose the perverse relationship including her role as a participant and then accomplice in the disavowal of a true learning relationship for an "academic" role or personality. These modes of relating and bearing witness occur all the time in our classrooms. The writing rubric is just one example.

I could also tell this story another way, as a masochistic version of the perverse relationship, where the teacher allows herself to be disciplined by the institution via the script/the rubric. She tries to say her lines perfectly, but it's never quite good enough. The tone is off. The emphasis is misplaced. She takes pleasure in trying to get it right the next time. She creates over and over again an institution intent on humiliating her, but the institution is never quite humiliating enough to satisfy her. To identify this pattern is to create the "thirdspace" for acts of improvisation in the classroom. As we stated earlier in this chapter, improvisations are the impromptu actions that Holland et al. claim allow for new, more responsive identities. Improvising (truly responding to the shifting conditions of our classrooms and our students) our way out of the masochistic script legitimates new institutional identities and rituals. This is not just a one-time affair, however. Collectively and institutionally placing value on improvisation and creating space for it empowers both teachers and students as decision makers within a vibrant, public sphere.

Us: We realized this might be a good place to offer several counternarratives or improvisations outside the institution/teacher, teacher/student binaries. Although we discuss in more detail in Chapter 4 how writing teachers might encourage students to create public spaces through various technologies and forums and through creative practices that challenge the forces of academic specialization and consumerist culture, Michelle does recommend the following counterstrategies in order to help teachers begin to imagine alternative classroom practices. One strategy asks students, when analyzing academic audiences, to take into account their audience's growing private interests.

Michelle: Many classroom and community practices do work to expose these secret contracts and unmask the institution or the teacher for what they really are in all their contingent, subjective, contradictory humanness. These pedagogies encourage inquiry into the academic audience as a group of people with various self-interests, secret deals, sets of assumptions, and interests that are becoming increasingly privatized, as well as private. While privacy is a more general term referring to an individual's freedom from outside observation, the process of privatization changes the spaces of public decision making (about education, the environment, resources, and law enforcement) into private, corporate-owned spaces. Privatization allows corporations an individual's right to privacy, that is, the right to keep decision-making processes that affect the public private. When institutions become privatized, no longer accountable to "the public," they (and their partners in the perverse relationship) become even more isolated and constricted. For example, with severe drops in state funding, public universities are contracting buildings, research programs, curricula, and testing to corporations and raising the tuition sometimes by 7.1 percent. Graham Spanier, president of Pennsylvania State University, told the *New York Times* in 2005 that increased tuition was a result of "public higher education's slow slide toward privatization" (Dillon 2005, 12). With the decrease in state funding and the increase in tuition, the relationship between the university and the public (with the university serving the "public good") becomes a relationship between the university and the individual student (with the university supplying a commodity to a consumer). In contracting curricula and programs to corporations, again the university is less accountable to the public (taxpayers, governmental agencies, and community groups) and more accountable to corporate interests. At UC Berkeley, for example, corporate employees sit on grant review boards alongside faculty members and administrators.

In the face of these powerful moves toward the privatization of our public resources, how can we as teachers engage in classroom and community practices that create spaces for public and collective decision making? The perverse relationship demands that any disparity, any differing viewpoints be downplayed. True learning, however, involves the public interest; it requires the Other in the form of the diverse public to create new knowledge and understanding. What if I, a teacher who sometimes hides behind her rubric (a rubric that is attached to an outcomes-based assessment program, which packages the ability to write and the English language as a university commodity, which is attached to the university's accreditation and ranking and recruitment procedures), decide to unmask my own subjectivity and the subjectivity of the university and open it up for discussion? I'm thinking of Victor Villanueva's syllabus anthologized in *Strategies for Teaching First-Year Composition*, where, in place of a grading rubric, he states, "The grading in this course is largely subjective" (2002, 100). Such a statement would require that the students, teacher, and institution allow themselves to be known and learn and know another inside and outside the conditioning of "school behavior." It would also require that students writing for an academic audience understand that audience as an institution with its own shifting and contradictory economic and political interests. We, as writing teachers, could also go beyond teaching our students how to write for public audiences (out there somewhere) and teach them how to create public audiences and spaces. Strategies for creating public spaces where multiple viewpoints are addressed, where decision-making processes are made transparent, are addressed in a number of disciplines from communication studies to political science.

Lil: What happens if the student, not the teacher, engages in a secret contract with the institution?

Michelle: Of all the secret contracts, the ones between the student and the institution are the least recognized and understood. Here's a second classroom profile that might make them more apparent and available for interpretation and improvisation. Educator Herbert Kohl identifies his students engaged in a common perverse relationship that is largely not witnessed by teachers, one where students wage a silent war of wills with the institution. When his students consistently failed to do the assigned coursework, Kohl looked more closely at their larger motivations beyond a simple dislike of the subject or himself and concluded that "[t]hey had consciously placed themselves outside the entire system that was trying to coerce or seduce them into learning and spent all their time and energy in the classroom devising ways of not-learning, shortcircuiting the business of failure altogether" (1994, 7). In Kohl's account, his students are not "failing"; they are perversely disavowing their needs and desires to know and investing in a secret contract with the school. Kohl, acting as the third party, chooses not to "remediate" or ignore these students but continuously and openly acknowledges their games, their choices to not-learn, and understands their stances toward learning as embedded within their choices about their own lives and identities. Kohl asks, Who is stuck? The student or the institution, with its single way of learning? I suggest both are stuck in a perverse relationship, alleviated only by the teacher's witness.

Mary Ann: Michelle, I think the prospect of "breaking the contract" of secrecy about the prescribed "relationships, bodies, and desires" that are enacted within the institution as you describe it is dangerous stuff. It is dangerous because it seeks to resist privatization and its push to commodify all public space to private interests. And yet what else can we do, from an ethical viewpoint? This may be what I'm getting at with my sense of limitations regarding alphabetic literacy—how certain notions of literacy are enacted as "perverse" relationships in the classroom and in the institution. When you make the distinction between the secret contract as perverse and not the institution itself, I think I'd make a similar distinction about alphabetic literacy and the "secret contracts" that are part of its social enactment. I don't necessarily think that the written word is, in and of itself, the creator of patriarchy. I guess I'd have to say the same thing about institutions—they are not inherently oppressive, patriarchal, or otherwise unethical. What you're saying, Michelle, is in fact the opposite—that writing brings the potential for breaking the secret contract, for pointing to (naming?) the assumptions that limit, even control, the narratives by which we live. And I totally agree with that, even as I struggle with a way for articulating what the limits and controls of alphabetic literacy are in the first place. (And I probably need a definition of alphabetic literacy at this point!)

I'm trying to find a way to talk about what might constitute a literacy that is not alphabetic but that operates by symbols other than words. This is where I found *The Alphabet Versus the Goddess: The Conflict Between Word and Image* interesting. The problem with it is not only the fairy tale of a world of goddess goodness before the written word and patriarchy, as Lil pointed out, but also the implication that the written word is inherently flawed, an instrument of oppression. The author himself (I did skip to the end) acknowledges the irony of making this argument even as he's writing this book. And of course he doesn't have an answer for his own contradictory actions. But still, I think that word and image may be set into opposition to each other when it comes to "secret contracts" in literacy instruction, similar to how language and action are dichotomized.

And at this point I am just going to grandly speculate (it's late, so that's a good thing to do before bed) that the secret contracts of alphabetic literacy insist that we do not experience words as materially constituted, as embodying sounds, rhythms, sensations of all sorts that affect us not only conceptually but physically, emotionally, spiritually, and socially. Instead, the secret contract is to blind, deafen, and otherwise deaden our embodied experience of language so that it does not speak back to us, does not offer ourselves an image of our own embodiment, individually as well as collectively. A secret contract in alphabetic literacy is to deaden us to the potential power of words, a power Michelle is saying is possible to regenerate by breaking the contract.

MARY ANN: I realize now, nearly a year and a half later, that this "secret contract" of literacy is yet another manifestation of the effects of privatization. Privatization, along with secrecy, depends upon a social contract that stipulates certain "secrets" as "normal" (in the sense that Michelle uses it) and thus invisible or hidden from public view. "Secret contracts" are what constitute the social construction of "reality." To see the secrets of how that construction is made is to make public that it is a secret in the first place and not just "normal" reality. Or, to go back to our earlier discussion, exposing the secret contract is an operation similar to an antifiction, showing the "seams" behind the seamless (social) fiction/construct that is represented as unquestionably "whole." Antifiction (at its best) creates spaces for readers to participate in the story's construction, which is what we are attempting to do in writing this dialogue—to offer readers spaces to participate in our dialogue, metaphorically if not literally. Of course, there's no guarantee that simply "showing the seams" of a story, even that of privatization's social construction, will change the perverse (commodified) relationships in the classroom. But such exposure does work toward creating public space in that it enables other representations of what was previously assumed to be "normal" to be articulated. By reading our dialogue, readers may better locate their own stories.

Somehow I want to talk about what I learned when I watched a drummer/poet with extensive knowledge of West African history and culture teach a group of small-town Indiana kids in a high school music room about how to "communicate" with drums. How, in a sense, I was not so much his third party as he was mine. And that his work is the kind we who teach alphabetic literacy need to support and learn from to find the "ethical agency" within literacy instruction. I'm not sure yet how this connects with what we've been saying so far, but I wanted to put it out there so you know I'm not speaking just abstractly about image versus word but have learned from this drummer who has done the kind of "pointing to" and naming that Michelle describes.

Good night!

Lil: Before you go into your story of the drummer, Mary Ann, can you say more about why you see breaking the secret contract as dangerous work for teachers?

Mary Ann: First off, consider the examples of Elizabeth Ito and Jay Bennish from Chapter 1. Ito broke the secret contract that says teachers are neutral delivery systems of information, information that comes from "objective" sources such as textbooks and newspapers. Because she dared to present a public position on a very public event—the war in Iraq—she was fired. Bennish broke a similar contract in his remarks about George W. Bush as president. He challenged assumptions about the classroom as "private" space, space that does not allow for the unknown, what Soja calls "thirdspace," in its ability to "[envision] a complex totality of potential knowledges but rejects any totalization that finitely encloses knowledge production in 'permanent structures' or specialized compartments/ disciplines" (1996, 57). He was not fired but he was given warning that next time he crossed this line, he most likely would be.

Lil: It is interesting to me that Bennish mentions in his letter to parents (see Appendix A) how he is creating a "safe" (public) space for his students, but he does not mention himself. His introductory statement claims the "space" as your history teacher—both the parents and the student. But then in the second sentence, he takes possession of the class, calling it "my class" rather than "our" class. So Sean Allen, in taping the class as proof of Allen's position, was opening up the dialogue to his father. Sean Allen's taping of the class could have been proof both of his "comfort" and "discomfort" in sharing ideas: comfort in that he felt free to tape record the classroom and share that tape with his father and discomfort in that he did not know how in Bennish's classroom to make his conservative viewpoint have the same weight as it did "outside."

Michelle: When Mary Ann and I interviewed Bennish, he told us Sean Allen had asked him what he thought about the State of the Union Address that day in class and that Bennish naively answered him in good faith as he would any student who expressed interest in a current event. This verifies Lil's assessment that Sean Allen was comfortable baiting and taping Bennish but was uncomfortable in expressing his own viewpoint. Since then, the school district has made it a policy that any student can tape any class without asking the permission of the teacher or students. It's difficult to know whether this policy is intended to provide students with the means for "agency" or "dialogue" or if it is intended to appease parents. I wonder what would have happened if Bennish had allowed students to co-write the letter to the parents or come up with course policies together. Even so, each student will have a different investment in the course's "master narrative"— whether that narrative encourages representation of multiple points of view or covering key facts within a subject. These investments help students construct an identity within what Holland et al. call the "cultural world," in this case of the classroom. Allen chose to disidentify with Bennish's narrative, choosing to follow a different set of rules and expectations.

Us: While Jay Bennish graciously granted Michelle and Mary Ann an interview in September 2007, and even commented on a previous draft of Chapters 1 and 2, we authors wish to acknowledge the constraints we all faced in creating space for Bennish to self-represent within our text. Like most classroom teachers, Bennish has neither the time nor the incentive to participate in a project such as ours. That is exactly the point we wish to make— Bennish's "absence" in our text illustrates the problem that all teachers of writing face when they lack the public space to self-represent. However, by interviewing Jay and committing ourselves to representing his perspective and engaging it as fairly as possible, we have tried our best to address the lack of economic resources, professional rewards, and time that privatization has placed upon us all. Such constraints continue to discourage dialogue, collaboration, and teacher-research across institutional and grade boundaries. We thank Jay Bennish for the time and attention he has provided us and hope our book will help him and other teachers and students continue in their struggle for public space. While you may not agree with Bennish's teaching approach or his responses to the press, we hope you will read his story as an example of what happens when all parties ignore (to varying degrees) the power relations created by school systems, cultural hierarchies, and private corporate interests.

Lil: Or, Michelle, was Allen following "the rules" as he understood them from the common sense view of "fair and balanced" as defined by Fox News? I'm wondering about the "master narrative" that constructs the classroom as "safe"—a site where I'm OK and you're OK—and everyone is entitled to his or her opinion. Public space is risky space and we enter that space to examine those ideas we take for granted. Doesn't "learning" mean "changing our minds?" If we see Bennish's classroom as what Holland and her co-authors call a "figured cultural world"—a world that constructs narratives that students and teachers live within and against, the Bennish narrative of "safe" and "comfortable" needs to be unpacked both for students and teachers.

Mary Ann: Bennish's students did not necessarily see him as lacking a viewpoint or position, or in other words, as "safe." But that does not necessarily mean that many of them did not find a certain freedom, if not safety, in the spaces of that classroom. Sean Allen clearly saw Bennish as upholding a particular viewpoint, one that was liberal and that made his own conservative positions "unsafe" in that environment. I agree with Lil's statement that Sean Allen's "discomfort" may well have been because his viewpoints did not hold the same weight or power in that classroom as they did in the right-wing media. In this regard, Allen is right that Bennish shows a bias—his bias was to create a classroom in which conservative viewpoints could not dominate unchallenged. However, Bennish's statements to his class that he wishes to create a "safe" environment and to the press that he engages "Devil's advocate" role playing don't represent what really happens in Bennish's classroom. Instead, what he says is strategic, addressing the requirements of school board curriculum. And therein lies the problem: He is left with so little room to claim public space as public space—not "safe" but free for all viewpoints to be represented and engaged. This does not mean, as Lil has said, that "I'm OK, you're OK" is the master narrative. Instead, it means one's positions are critically examined. Everyone has a stake; everyone (including the teacher) is subject to changing their minds. I wonder: Did Bennish include himself as subject to changing his mind?

Us: During their interview with Bennish, Michelle and Mary Ann asked him if he was also subject to changing his mind in the classroom, and he said, although it's rare, he does change his mind in response to his students' arguments. To what extent is any teacher truly compelled toward such self-reflexivity, especially when it is often the case that students' viewpoints are less well-developed than our own?

Lil: Bennish's example made me start to think about what we are teaching writing for: Bennish's publicly neutral position would equate with teaching writing as skill, just learn how to make an argument; it doesn't matter what you are saying, just say it correctly in the right format. If we are teaching writing for social change—so that people learn how to participate in academic/social/civic life—then *what* we write about matters and *how* we understand that *what* also matters. How we position our arguments in relation to others' views and positions also matter. The teacher must be positioned (she can't be the neutral gadfly) so that students understand reasoned debate and intellectual differences.

Michelle: I also have trouble with the notion of teacher neutrality. Teachers like Bennish represent themselves as neutral because institutions don't often have the vocabulary or space for the messy, tricky processes of real social engagement. Many institutions adopt the "liberal response" (for example, Michael Bérubé's argument of "procedural liberalism" [2006, 21]) to right-wing critics like David Horowitz and argue for a "liberal" classroom where a diversity of viewpoints is allowed and not one single viewpoint dominates. Maybe this shouldn't be an end in itself but part of a larger process. What gets lost in the "neutral classroom" is what you both indicate: a critical look at all viewpoints. Not all viewpoints are "okay." There are critical/ethical choices to be made on issues. Isn't bringing as many voices in as possible just one step in the critical-thinking, decision-making process? Patricia Roberts-Miller suggests that we get rid of the very notions of neutral or biased teaching (because they don't represent how arguments are made and deliberation is done in a vibrant public space) and concentrate instead on fairness (2004, 207).

Mary Ann: Bennish claims to hold to the idea of the "neutral" classroom, but it would appear he has no room to claim otherwise.

Lil: I think you hit the nail on the head, Mary Ann. I remember watching Bennish on the *Today Show*, and, while he was very articulate, I remember thinking that he had an opportunity to talk about "teaching," but, instead, he talked about being neutral in the classroom and being misrepresented in the press. It got me thinking about our part-time faculty who *always* stay neutral because they fear losing their jobs. In a neutral classroom, students don't learn the theoretical/philosophical underpinnings of various positions and the ethical implications of particular stances. They learn, "I'm OK, you're OK" and nothing changes.

Mary Ann: Bennish's apparently neutral stance, based solely on media representations of him, upholds the conventional view of objectivity, the same one supported by the press that called him out for "disciplining." At the same time, he wasn't afraid to give his point of view. You might ask why Bennish responded to Allen's question about the State of the Union Address with such an analysis and claim that Bennish was straying from the facts, or objective reality, of geography and instead offering his own interpretations on geopolitical issues and events. But when asked by reporters if his class was really about geography, Bennish explained that geography wasn't just about places and names and dates, but named a host of "geographies," including political, cultural, economic, as well as spatial. He noted that the class in question was an introductory lecture to concepts and terms he would be working with later.

Whether you agree with Bennish's representation of geography, one thing is clear: Disagreement and diverse views on what constitutes a subject area are, in the minds of most scholars, exactly what makes a discipline a discipline. Disciplinary boundaries are argued over, drawn and redrawn as new approaches, new subjects, and new perspectives come into play. The fact that Jay Bennish represents geography in these broader, more interpretive terms is less a reflection of his personal bias or opinion and more one of the state of the discipline overall. And, as most scholars agree, it is important to have the space, materially, discursively, and imaginatively, for a discipline—in the words of the poem that appear at the beginning of Chapter 1: to *breathe*. To regard the work of scholarship as simply a collection of the dead wood of facts is to deny its living presence as fire, fires that fuel imagination, change, and transformation with the knowledge of the past.

LIL: Every day on my way to work in the English department at UNC Charlotte, I'm visually assaulted by the statue that is mounted in front of the main public entrance to the building. The statue is of a naked man, supposedly the archetypal student, rising triumphantly from stone. Neither I nor most students can escape the naked man statue. (Even my office window opens to it.) Yet because the statue is so "normal"—so "uncontroversial"—few people even notice him and even seem to accept the image uncritically. When I was agitating to redesign the statue, adding breasts or a brassiere, a student said to me, "Lil, you make too much out of this thing. You, know, I'm one of those campus tour guides, and they tell us to tell prospective students that the statue is supposed to be how every 'man' forms himself through education—creates himself as it were." The fact that no man creates himself alone—not in education, not in life—was no argument in the face of the common sense, my response to her was, "If he is doing this creation-thing alone, where did the chisel come from?"

This naked man creation myth participates in the same American mythos that constructs the students' identities in our Bennish tale. The Ragged Dick–bootstraps narrative, the rags to riches tale, the story that if one really tries hard enough in America he can make it on his own, serves simultaneously to eliminate the role of women and teachers in the construction of students and teachers and to make invisible that teaching/learning are social and should be public.

Mary Ann: So, let's apply Lil's question to her own teaching story. What were the risks involved in breaking her secret contract? Perhaps one risk for her as she attempted to act as third-party witness to the violence enacted between her students and the institutions they must submit to was for her to be recast in the classroom narrative as someone who "simply 'talks'" but who is incapable of action, who, like the victims of such violence, are too fearful to fight back. Like Michelle, I'm wondering how Lil made the case about the violence of words and physical violence, but I'm guessing that the very act of making arguments may have worked against her as much as for her.

In a sense, the alphabetic literacy that we rely so much on as part of our "academic personality," one that separates logic from emotion, ideas from bodies, and rationality from creativity, has placed her into a kind of pedagogical catch-22. The students are claiming that words have no real power over people—to control dangerous situations, to provide amenities. Words are cast as maternal artifacts. They're what one uses when one can't *do* anything. So in Lil's using words to make her case—to break the contract of secrecy by calling "normal" behavior "violent"—she simply reinscribes her maternal powerlessness, that is, all talk and no action. She talks because (implicitly) she *can't* act. She can't "discipline" them into accepting her argument. (Or so they think.) And thus, they don't have to (and perhaps won't) listen to her. The violence here is that she is silenced, at least in this moment. Or, at least that's how I read her narrative.

Of course she isn't silenced in terms of her retelling the story or in asking her students to speak and write more about violence, offering new texts and materials that recontextualize the "perverse" relationship the students are in with the institution. Lil can't "make" them examine their views, but chances are they would, because she does, after all, have the power of the grade. But whether they do it through passive resistance (just going through the motions) or whether she actually does assist them in "breaking the contract" is another matter. The power of the grade is still part of alphabetic literacy (even grades are assigned as letters!) and as such, has limited power in a world in which such literacy is both reified as a disciplinary power (something they must submit to or feel the pain of correction) and denigrated as "just talk" (something that can't, ultimately, address their deepest desires, needs, or, as Michelle says, "libidinal investments").

The other side to this "perverse" or "secret" contract is that in making her arguments, Lil is aligning herself with the institution and the paternal/patriarchal powers that her students are arguing are necessary. Literacy itself may just be "more talk" but if, as Stuckey says, "the teaching of literacy . . . is a regulation of access," Lil is still a gatekeeper. Her students identify with having gatekeepers. The victim identifies with her abuser. So her students identify with her power and at the same time see it as located elsewhere.

Lil's story is just one story of thousands we construct about our literacy classrooms in our professional lives. In the context of so many stories we tell, this one might, on one hand, seem very low risk. What did you, Lil, put on the line, really? She's tenured, promoted twice, and solidly established in her career. So what could possibly be risky for Lil in this scene?

MARY ANN: Flashback to the Fall 2004 semester, and I'm teaching another advanced fiction writing class, this time with a focus on collaboration in writing. I have framed the course around breaking a "secret contract" in how writing identities are shaped—namely the dichotomy between individual and collective authorship, texts, processes, and influences. In addition to the usual activities of drafting, discussing, and revising stories for a final portfolio, we read three collaboratively written books of fiction (two novels and a collection of interwoven stories), write a collaborative class novel, and present group projects on collaborative process.

Anticipating resistance regarding doing collaborative writing (especially for a grade), I stress, in the syllabus and in class, how the point of the class isn't to learn how to write collaboratively but to see how collaboration is already part of what they do (in other words, the "secret contract" that I wish to make public) and to work with more awareness of what forms collaboration takes in their work as writers. I seek to break the contract of privatized notions of authorship (individual voice and style exist as separate and unique, outside the social), of labor (great writers work alone), of free-market forces (great works are those published by corporate entities and enshrined in institutional canons).

I tell my students I want them to take risks for the sake of learning, even if it means their writing gets "worse." I am not prepared for what kind of "risks" they do, in fact, take. I am not prepared for "losing control"—or, upon reflection, realizing how much I expect to be "in control." During the last week of classes, the last group of three performs its collaborative project. The week before, the group included me in its discussion of what they would do: stage a mock argument as they entered class, then ask their classmates to write individual accounts of what they saw. They saw these accounts as their entrée into a conversation about perception and collaborative process.

The key to this performance was to keep it a secret. No one would know it was an "act" until after it was over.

After the performance, the group acknowledged that keeping this secret was not necessary to generating this discussion. So why did they choose to keep this secret? And why did I agree to let them do so?

The performance: Two of the four males in this group enter class bickering. The only female rolls her eyes, shoves at the one male's shoulder, and tells them to knock it off. The other two males mostly just watch. (During the next class period, as we discuss the outcomes of this performance, several students note how such bickering and shoving seemed "normal" for this group.) I begin class, expecting that the performance is over. I am about to turn the class over to them. But before I can, the two males who entered bickering are now glaring at each other from across the room. They interrupt me with angry words, swearing at each other. Then they leap from their desks and start assaulting each other, rolling on the floor.

Of course it is an act. Isn't it? Part of me assumes it isn't real. But another part of me freezes, as I did as a child when confronted by such violence. Another student, an older male, rises out of his seat, shouting to break up the fight. Part of me thinks he's in on the act; part of me knows he thinks it's real. Another student (also male) angrily asks the group in question if this is just an act. When they say yes, he leaves the room, too shaken (and perhaps angry) to stay.

The next forty-eight hours are spent in processing this event: I talk to the group after class, send and receive emails from the two men who responded to the "fight" and one from a female student who is also shaken by what happened. We spend most of the class, our final meeting for the semester, continuing to discuss what happened. The group apologizes; I insist that they also say what they think they did wrong, after apologizing myself and saying what I did wrong, namely to keep the secret.

While this is not an experience I wish to repeat, it underscores quite dramatically the need to break such secret contracts. In keeping this secret, the group and I were refusing to acknowledge our collaboration with the rest of the class. The group's collaboration broke down because of this secret, enabling the two men to turn to an enactment of physical violence as the best way to make their point.

In individual exit conferences, I did not hesitate to point out how essential collaboration is, given the consequences of its failure. We all felt the consequences, although some more painfully than others. It was a teachable moment, but hardly the kind that are in the canon of "permissible" stories. At least I haven't heard or read one like this.

Michelle: But aren't most teaching experiences performances like this one? Perhaps the shock and violence is not as extreme, but doesn't coercion and control depend upon unspoken agreements about who has authority and credibility and who doesn't?

Lil: Yes, and I still want Mary Ann to address the risks of making those secret agreements public in the classroom.

Mary Ann: I've felt the push-pull of this apparent contradiction for a long time, of positioning myself inside alphabetic literacy to teach it and as breaking its contract of secret "regulation of access." It's not just one scene like this but many that have accumulated over the years. I have clung to David Bartholomae's phrase, "within and against," one that, by the way, came via you, Lil, as a kind of mental life raft and compass (2007, 392). But I also felt that it didn't help me understand its enactment, how to move through such contradictory positions, to embody them in ways that would not tear me to pieces in the oppositional discourses that underlie literacy instruction. To even understand that there was a way to move that embodied such contradictions was a big step in my search for a "third-party" witness—in this case, a community arts youth outreach group focused on nonviolent education. Through them, and through my own personal bodywork, I began to understand that the habits of mind, the mental moves that are part of the secret contracts of literacy, can be reformed—and perhaps, without the high stakes Michelle is rightly identifying. The risk, at this point, is of my "academic identity," something I can't live without, but I can't really live with, either, not as it is currently constructed institutionally. Specifically, the risk is that I am breaking a contract of mind set in opposition to body, of logic against emotion, of intellect against sexuality, a contract that I should add has served me pretty well, too. The risk is not only from the outside but from within. It's about being heard.

So I guess I'm saying, yeah, there are risks. But I still feel hopeful that in doing what Michelle is suggesting, breaking these contracts via narrative or other "embodied" forms of literacy, making them, as we have been emphasizing, "public," that new, more equitable contracts can be written, new identities scripted that are more expansive, that stand to give us more "breathing space."

Michelle: But why should our students risk engaging in such dialogues? As Erica McWilliam asks in "Beyond the Missionary Position: Teacher Desire and Radical Pedagogy," why should our students risk anything including "an immune system built for late capitalism?" A critical, embodied pedagogy engages with actual people and bodies who often fight for their servitude "as stubbornly as though it were their salvation." These individuals, including our own students and colleagues, are not "'innocent dupes' but are enacting most powerfully the perversion of desire—they may genuinely want the fascism" and quick fixes of late capitalism, to sacrifice the body to the mind, to cast aside the messy literacies of materialism and lived experience (1997, 222). "Thus," as McWilliam notes, "our [radical pedagogical] project is always at risk because it is not lived abstractly but is embodied in the continuous production of real desiring identities in institutions of learning" (1997, 229). Whatever form the pedagogy takes, however, a teacher who takes part in pedagogical events is forced to confront the limits of her own anatomical body, her own erotic experiences of learning and teaching, as well as her disciplinary "bodies" of knowledge. Where do we find the rub? Barthes writes, "What I hide in my language, my body utters. . . . My body is a stubborn child, my language is a very civilized adult" (1977, 45).

MARY ANN: In my fiction class last night, our first night of the semester, we were discussing the conventions of introductions (literally to each other in class but then later textual introductions in works of fiction). We talked about taboos of being "too personal" or "too intimate" although we all recognized how much more interesting the more "personal" intros usually were. One female student described how, in another class, another female student announced that she had been violently raped as her opening introduction on the first day of class. After that, other students shunned her, except the one who told our class this story. We talked about what the student who had been raped accomplished by telling such a story about herself, the protective, self-defensive gesture in that revelation. There is also the question of what is at stake in disrupting unspoken conventions of discourse—that many may shun you, but at the same time you create an audience, however small, of those who "get" you and will offer support. And then there is, of course, the matter of self-representation and the power this student claimed in making rape a public, political matter, not something for her to hide behind in "personal" shame. The fact that other students shunned her and the teacher could barely stammer out an answer suggests a lot in terms of our cultural responses to rape and to the telling of rape stories in public. I don't mean to condemn anyone for their personal responses, for I surely would have been stunned as well; I don't know how responsive I could have been at that moment. Yet this story was a good one for talking about how disrupting conventions can be meaningful in ways that we don't always understand, that we tend to resist because we don't see such gestures as meaningful, as acts of self-representation. Instead, we try to erase them as "crazy" or "too emotional" or otherwise inappropriate.

While I don't see it as my role to require my students to self-disclose and thus take risks they may not be prepared to take, that story makes me start to think about alternative narratives to a culture in which a woman is compelled to take such a risk to, paradoxically, make herself feel safe. Lil, this reminds me a bit of the Lynn Z. Bloom narrative you critiqued at CCCC one year, where the only alternatives offered in Lynn's narrative were to submit to her assaulter or to run naked and screaming into the night. I don't blame this woman for screaming, naked, in her classroom introduction. I do, however, question a world in which she felt compelled to do so. She clearly felt the classroom as a place that could, potentially, reproduce her rape experience and so acted accordingly. In a sense, keeping rape narratives "private" serves a similar function as the naked man statue and the Ragged Dick—bootstraps stories, namely to keep the knowledge of those who labor to maintain the conventional systems of knowledge invisible, including the violence used to maintain that invisibility (rape being one example). To see teachers as also knowledge makers, and researchers/ scholars as engaged in learning and teaching is to seriously disrupt that narrative by disrupting the hierarchies of the division of labor. It may be that we "expose" ourselves and risk further acts of violence, like shunning, in this sort of disruption. But as Amy Vidali suggests, it is possible for those who are labeled as cultural "freaks" to "manipulate both existing and unexpected rhetorical tropes for their own ends" (2007, 616).

Us: We wish there were a way to capture the silences, the days of no response, the exercises in restraint that we each experienced. This book has been in process for years. Our dialogues have been cut short by deaths, illnesses, travel, work, trauma, and joy. Rather than this seamless, ongoing dialogue, our actual "conversations" are punctuated with long silences, with gaps and forgetfulness, as much as any sustained coherence. This is where the form itself privatizes the challenges of maintaining any sense of dialogue, of creating public spaces for us to engage each other. But this is also where writing itself enables such spaces. We could and subsequently did go back and fill in, rewrite, and reflect on what we initially composed. We created coherence, found new and better ways to represent ourselves as we progressed. But it was not without some struggle. Yet in our struggle we found rewards in re-visioning how we know what we knew, or to paraphrase Ann Berthoff, finding out what we thought by seeing what we said, over and over again (1978, 154). Because we were writers, we could always come back to our words, no matter where our lives took us in between.

Endnote

1. Since 2003, Mary Ann has collaborated with the Three Rivers Jenbe Ensemble, a cultural outreach group focusing on West Afrikan drumming and dance for young people in Fort Wayne, Indiana. She teaches creative writing as part of their broader curriculum. Her university students may elect a service learning option as part of a class Mary Ann designed specifically for this purpose, Creativity and Community.

3 | Challenging the Private Boundaries of the Discipline

A Play

In the previous two chapters, we have discussed as well as performed the effects of privatization on writing instruction to engage teachers of writing in exactly what is at stake and how public space matters, not only within but also beyond the writing classroom. In this chapter, we continue with our performance of the struggle for public space, this time in the form of a play. Composition scholar Nedra Reynolds has written how the material conditions of the Conference on College Composition and Communication (CCCC) shape the larger discourse of the field of composition studies. She argues, "Many of the debates, discussions and conversations about writing instruction take place in hotels or on conference sites distinguished by huge buildings in the downtown areas of major cities" (1998, 32). The conference, she continues, "requires 35 contiguous meeting rooms and 1,500 sleeping rooms for a four-day gathering of over 3,000 members. . . . While the effort to rotate the locations by region has been in place for years, increasing efforts to accommodate political concerns have made the process of site selection fraught with difficult decisions about 'whose' interests count more or which cities have the least offensive laws or statutes" (32).

Reynolds notes that there are also "many small material realities that affect many things about the success of a conference site. . . . [W]hen we are occupied with transportation woes, the cost of a meal in a hotel, or the lack of women's bathroom stalls, time and energy are taken away from conversations about writing, about students, about our programs and ideas" (33). In addition, "meeting in hotels does mean that workers must serve and clean up after us" (33).

While Reynolds analyzed these conditions—or to use Soja's term, *spaces*—using the genre of critical essay, we will address them using the genre of fictionalized drama, which allows us to re-stage our various conference experiences in order to make visible and thus public some of the repressed material (thoughts, emotions, and desires, as well as the material and economic conditions) fueling our performances. By dramatizing Reynolds' claim, we wish to show how the available spaces and forms for talk within the conference structure (e.g., the hotel-restaurant franchise and its architecture, disciplinary specialization, and so on) shape not only professional discourse but also participants' sense of identification as professionals in very specific, material ways, most notably by forces of privatization.

Privatization, as we discussed in Chapter 1, drives not only material, economic, and political decisions and events, but in more fundamental ways governs what is visible and thus "real" within the social realm. If power depends upon invisibility to have the greatest impact, then privatization fuels the habits that most effectively shield what is powerful from public scrutiny and access. In the following play, we seek to dramatize the processes by which privatization influences how professional identities and, in turn, professional discourse are embodied (or, to use Soja's term, *spatialized*) as well as disembodied for the sake of maintaining a hierarchy of power.

This chapter is a fictional account, not a re-enactment, of a session at the 2003 CCCC. At CCCC that year, of the three authors, only Mary Ann was actually at the conference in New York. Michelle was stuck in Denver after a snowstorm dumped seventeen inches on the city, and Lil was home because of her daughter's concerns about terrorism. (Bush had officially declared war on Iraq that week.) The three of us, with Nancy Welch, had planned to present a panel (written as an ongoing dialogue among us) titled "Feminist Rewritings of the (Body) Politic." Instead,

Mary Ann and Nancy read their parts, while two volunteers read the contributions of Lil and Michelle. What we represent here is not that particular presentation, but a fictionalized version, with fictionalized characters, of a presentation that *could have* taken place given our various experiences in such venues. We have made ourselves into characters in order to add thoughts and feelings and images that run through our minds as we "present" the material, a method we hope will illuminate our political and economic motivations and the motivations of the other characters in this drama—the audience, the questioners, the room, and the location itself.

Feminist scholar Nancy Tuana creates a similar fictionalized dialogue in *Feminist Interpretations of Plato* where she and her colleague, William Cowling, "attempt to subvert contemporary philosophical narratives that privilege a disembodied, authorial voice by casting the study as a performance and employing a multiplicity of voices" (1994, 138). Their dialogue performs the presence and absence of the feminine in Plato and contemporary philosophical discourse. Like Tuana's and Cowling's, our drama will show conflict between the speakable and unspeakable, what is rewarded and what is punished, in the scene of a composition studies conference presentation. It will perform the presence and absence of the body—its materiality and emotions—in the discourse of our field. As we argued in the previous two chapters, privatization can create and reinforce disembodied forms of knowing, enacting a violent separation of the body from language and discourse. Our play will demonstrate the silencing and disciplining effects of the secret contracts (unstated, taken-for-granted agreements about who gets to speak about what and how and where) that maintain our field's boundaries and the larger forces of privatization by exposing and disrupting them.

We include minor details such as clothing, personal habits and preferences, and other character traits to illustrate how these constitute the concrete material choices we make in order to create an image of professionalism and a sense of belonging to the field of composition. These choices affect not only our own and others' perceptions but the material well-being of countless workers and economic systems. Although untrue to actual events and people, our play is rooted in the actual issues and material conditions we, the profession, the nation, and the world were—and in many respects still are—experiencing at that time.

FEMINIST REWRITINGS OF THE (BODY) POLITIC

Characters (in order of appearance)

Speaker, LIL: A full professor at a research university in the South. Her work is primarily in the area of writing and English education. She is white and in her early fifties, with streaked blonde hair cut and curled in layers around her face. She's wearing a loose-fitting linen pantsuit and gold jewelry with her initials in lacy script.

Speaker, MICHELLE: An assistant professor at an urban university in the West. Her work is primarily in the area of gender and writing technologies. She's white and in her mid-thirties, with short dark brown hair, parted to the side, tapered loosely around the ears and back. She's wearing a black polyester/rayon, flared, short skirt and a sleeveless forest green polyester/nylon shell with black sequins around the collar.

Speaker, MARY ANN: An associate professor at an urban university in the Midwest. Her work focuses on narrative, gender, and writing. White and in her mid-forties, she wears a light green Italian wool dress with a funnel neck and A-line skirt that hits just above her knees. Her red hair is cut in layers to just above her shoulders. Silver rings with gemstones mark the middle three fingers on each hand.

Responder, "JANE": An associate professor at a research university in Florida. Her work primarily addresses the effects of social and economic class on the teaching of writing. She is white and in her late forties, with blond hair cut in a bob, and is wearing a light brown pantsuit and black, heavy-rimmed glasses.

Questioner 1, "GREG": A "name" in the field, he is a full professor at a research university in California. His work focuses on radical pedagogy in composition studies. He is white and in his mid-fifties, with short light brown and gray hair, and is wearing dark blue jeans, a white shirt, a tweed jacket, and rimless glasses.

Questioner 2, "CHERYL": A nontenured lecturer, who teaches four classes a semester, plus directs a writing center. Her work focuses on research in teaching and tutoring writing to diverse student populations. She is a woman of color, with light brown wavy hair that touches her shoulders. She's in her mid-thirties and wears navy blue pants with a red and navy printed silk blouse.

Questioner 3, "TESSA": A female tenure-track assistant professor at a mid-sized university in the Appalachian Mountains. Her work focuses on cognitive and neuroscientific models of composition. She's wearing a forest green sleeveless cotton dress and a tailored black denim jacket. She's white and in her early thirties, with long curly blond hair.

Other conference participants

Act I

The scene is the Conference on College Composition and Communication in New York, March 21, 2003. As the curtain rises, we see a rectangular hotel conference meeting room with high ceilings, thick, dark carpeting, taupe walls, and fifty cushioned, straight-backed chairs arranged in rows of ten with an aisle down the middle.

The audience's view is from the back of this room, where approximately fifteen people are already seated. Some are sitting alone, leafing through their conference schedules, while others are in pairs, talking to one another, their voices muffled by the carpeting and high ceilings. Every few seconds another person or cluster of people enters the room from one of the double doors stage right. Each time the door opens, the animated sounds of hallway conversations disrupt for a moment the hushed tones of the meeting room.

At the front of the room there is one long table and four chairs situated on a dais. On top of the table is a podium with a microphone and three half-full pitchers of water, along with several empty glasses. The three speakers are seated at the table to the left of the podium, each reading over her notes. One hotel worker enters the room, fills the water pitchers and leaves three clean glasses upside down on the table. She takes the used glasses with her. A technical worker enters, tests the microphones and overhead projector, asks if the speakers need anything, and leaves.

After a few seconds of this scene unfolding, LIGHTS DIM THEN GO TO BLACK, *revealing* LIL, MARY ANN, *and* MICHELLE *in separate spotlights filtered in red, green, and blue, respectively. Each character stops what she was doing and pauses, looking in different directions, away from each other and the conference participants who were around them, out beyond the audience. This alternative scene lingers for a few moments until the first scene with full lighting gradually returns.*

LIL *walks over to* MICHELLE.

LIL: You about ready to get this show on the road, Michelle? I really love your outfit. Did you find it in Denver?

Lights dim then darken as blue spotlight shines on MICHELLE.

MICHELLE (*Facing the audience but speaking in a voice she expects only herself to hear*)**:** Both of these pieces come from a salvage store in southern Alabama. It's a small chain that sells liquidated merchandise from larger department stores, like Macy's and Bloomingdales, at a quarter or a tenth of the retail price. I really miss that store. I loved the way it let me look somewhat fashionable for one-tenth the price. After a hurricane in Florida, a flood in Louisiana, or a fire in California, the store would pick up lots of merchandise.

Outside the spotlight, a shadowed figure moves into the room through the double doors. MICHELLE *pauses, looks around, as if startled.*

I bet if Lil and Mary Ann knew where I got these threads, they would make me check on the store's buying, hiring, or work policies. I remember most of the workers were older women, women of color, with name tags like "Miss Ida Mae" or "Miss Caroline."

Lights come up as spotlight fades.

MICHELLE (*Turning to* LIL)**:** Thanks, Lil. Can't remember just where I got this. I'm ready to go.

LIL: Great. You ready, Mary Ann? (*She nods yes while fanning her face with one hand.*) At least *we* are. Holding a session at 8:30 in the morning is going to make a lot of folks think twice about coming. At least we're not on Saturday again. Why do we always seem to get scheduled on Saturdays for this conference?

As with MICHELLE, *lights dim and spotlight comes up on* LIL, *this one in red.*

LIL (*Facing the audience but speaking in a voice she expects only herself to hear*): I've attended this conference nearly every year for almost thirty years. At first everyone knew each other. We had common issues; we read each other's work. You could count on people coming to your panel, joining the discussion. Sparks would fly; ideas poured out. We were doing something really important, something that mattered.

She pauses, scans the audience, sighs.

Now it just feels so—so BIG. So easy to get lost in the crowd. And the funny thing is, just as these books and articles are being written like crazy, the publishers are pulling out. One university press flat out told us that our book, *Composing Public Space*, is just too risky. That they only published "established" names to make their sales. What happened to the days when university presses were the ones that could take the risks? They didn't have to worry so much about sales then. They were there to promote new ideas. What good is academic freedom when you have no place to publish?

Lights come up as spotlight fades.

MARY ANN (*Squinting, hand to brow*): Looks like a couple more just staggered in. I can't remember the last time I got up for an 8:30 session. Remember last year we were at 9:30? I thought *that* was early! (*To* MICHELLE *and* LIL): Does it feel hot in here to you? (*They shake their heads no.*) Maybe we should open a door.

A hotel worker, a middle-aged woman with large black-framed glasses and light brown, freckled skin, thrusts her head in through the door, swivels it to sweep her eyes across the room, then quickly withdraws, closing the door behind her after a long, pointed look at the front table where the panelists sit.

As with the other two panelists, lights dim and spotlight comes up on MARY ANN, this one in green.

MARY ANN (*Facing the audience but speaking in a voice she expects only herself to hear*): At least I can help keep the place clean. (*She wipes wet* *rings off the tablecloth before straightening the stack of glasses.*) Then again, I love staying in hotels because someone else makes the bed every morning. I love the clean, neatly folded towels—I can't fold for the life of me—and the little bottles of toiletries. I have a whole drawer full of nothing but hotel soaps, shampoo, and lotion, even shower caps. Heaven is someone else replacing the toilet paper. Oh, and those mints on the pillow and coffee pots right in the room.

She hears a noise outside the spotlight, looks around. Picks up the sweating water glass and eyes it carefully.

I wonder how many days these housekeepers would have to work to afford one night's stay here? Am I supposed to tip them? New Yorkers tip for everything, but my department's travel fund doesn't even come close to covering the airfare, let alone the room, meals, and taxis.

A cacophony of voices rises then falls outside the spotlight.

That reminds me. Two summers ago I did research in Chicago. I'd searched the Net for a bargain hotel rate. The "bargain" greeted me as I approached the hotel's door. To get inside, I'd have to cross a picket line of hotel workers. But I had no way of finding another room. Sheepishly, I crossed the line.

Last summer, I booked the "bargain" hotel again. Surely the strike was over. Guess what? Another picket line. And the city was full—a festival in Grant Park. I had no choice; I had no where else to stay. To ease my conscience, I talked to some of the picketers, young, energetic women from Colombia. They gave me a flyer with a website to check for hotels picketed by their union.

Lights come up as spotlight fades.

MARY ANN (*To conference participants*): Let's get started. Good morning. I'm Mary Ann Cain from Indiana University Purdue University Fort Wayne. Our panel today is a dialogue on "Feminist Rewritings of the (Body) Politic." Instead of three separate papers, we have written this as a continuous dialogue with each other. So be aware that there will be no breaks between speakers.

"Talk is cheap." Shirley Brice Heath turned this old chestnut on its head when she advocated having young learners study how and why people spoke the way they did. Talk *is* cheap, but that's the beauty of it; in its being cheap, it is ultimately priceless. We can't do without it. Yet so much of the "talk about talk" in the academy and in the political discourses of local, national, and global affairs would seem to claim otherwise. Talk is not only cheap, *the story goes,* but worthless in the face of violence. Language, both written and spoken, has little power to change the course of terror and terrorism in our daily lives. Action is set in opposition to language. If talk is cheap, then action "speaks louder than words."

If talk is cheap, then I'd argue that's because talk is associated with women and women's work. Women are always talking, and talking about a lot of nothing, or so the cultural narrative goes. The other side to this story is that men don't talk, or not much, but through their actions they "speak." And again, this is perceived to be the more effective mode. Talking isn't acting, and acting isn't talking. It isn't hard to see what is considered more powerful within our cultural contexts.

I want to challenge this cultural story by looking at narratives that depict language and action, and in particular, violence as a form of action, as pitted against each other in a struggle in which ultimately violence prevails. Embedded in these cultural narratives is the assumption that language is "merely" symbolic, having no material effects in and of itself, and that violence, having only material effects, is meaningless, or as media rhetoric goes, "senseless." Have you ever heard of violence called meaningful unless it's called by some other name—police action, national defense, discipline?

Feminists in the academy have a responsibility to draw attention to the more "politic" ways that the academy reinscribes these cultural narratives of violence, a violence that I argue is quite meaningful as well as strategic in its social, political, and economic aims. However, in doing so, we risk, at the very least, being shunned as "impolitic." Even more disturbing, as the following story from Nancy Welch suggests, we risk ourselves being singled out as targets of violence:

> I'm still shaky from the experience of having become visible to a group of young men on my campus. These young men hang posters proclaiming "Bomb Iraq Now." They are the authors of "web logs," or "blogs," which devote considerable space to railing against politically active women faculty. One blogger recently referred to me as a "stupid bitch" whose

"ass" should be "fired" for helping to organize a protest against Dinesh D'Souza. Another convinced a columnist from the city's newspaper to run a piece about "extremist faculty" whose anti-war views silence students, the columnist naming a colleague and me as prime, pernicious examples. Given that my colleague and I were both on sabbatical at the time, the charge took me by surprise, as did the phone call from another colleague who scolded, "How could you let yourself be talked about that way?" It's been an awakening to realize that I could be so visible to a group of young men I could not pick out on the street or identify in a line-up.

Actually I think it's because I have never met them that their words feel especially threatening, taking on muscle and weight, particularly when I'm crossing the campus after dark or working in my office on a Saturday afternoon. True, I am not subjected to the witch hunt that's recently deported Arab and Muslim students by the hundreds; I have not been publicly harangued as an anti-American foreigner as a friend was by Rush Limbaugh on his nationally syndicated radio program. I have tenure, a union, and a U.S. passport. These faceless bloggers haven't come up with words that can really hurt me. But it's also true, as Michael Moore's exposé *Bowling for Columbine* amply dramatizes, that violence in the United States is no social aberration. In this hyperimperialist moment, it's the norm, and the commands that these young men issue—*Bomb Iraq now, Fire her ass*—cannot be separated from their desire and ability to align themselves with those empowered to make such words so (2004).

MARY ANN: And to complicate things even further, we risk alienating other feminists whose pacifist ideals of cooperation, consensus building, and care can sometimes support the very discourses that maintain and regulate violence as a practice of academic "disciplining." Thus, the more "visible" we become in speaking out against violence and the sociopolitical agendas it supports, the more aware we become of how invisible those who drive this agenda are, sheltered by cultural conventions that govern authority and power.

MARY ANN *glances down at the "No Blood for Oil" button pinned on her imported wool dress, the one she got on sale from a catalogue whose trademark is its highly aestheticized descriptions of merchandise, then briefly pauses, self-conscious, and scans the room for signs of reaction. Sweat starts to bead on her forehead. She wipes it off unthinkingly.*

Lights dim; spotlight is on MARY ANN.

MARY ANN (*Distracted*): Why don't these places ever have windows that actually open? There's that saying, "If you can't stand the heat, get out of the kitchen." A friend of mine once changed it to say, "If you can't stand the heat, open a window." But if there are no windows, what are your choices? Like Nancy Welch, I want to make my positions on issues like the Iraq war public. I don't want to close off or "privatize" my academic self. Why should I hide it in a windowless room separate from my "public," civic self?

I tape *Make Jobs Not War* and *Bush Lies; Who Dies?* stickers to my office door, along with anti-war cartoons and articles. Unlike Nancy, the worst reaction was from a couple of students who wrote "rebuttals" in the margins of my postings. I can't totally blame them; even they are hungry for space to discuss and debate. And when the *Bush Lies* stickers disappear from my door—three times so far—I can only hope they've gone to a good home.

But I'm just one person. At times I feel too unprepared and vulnerable to face the anger, fear, or hate that is bound to come. So I wind up "disciplining" myself to sound more appeasing, less New York "in your face."

Lights come up as spotlight fades.

QUESTIONER 2 *raises her hand slowly and deliberately until* MARY ANN, *taken aback, notices.*

MARY ANN: Uh, you have a question? (*She looks at her watch.*) We timed our dialogue to allow for questions at the end.

QUESTIONER 2: Well, if you'd rather wait . . .

MARY ANN (*Glancing around*): To be honest—

QUESTIONER 3 (*Quickly standing*): You just said this is a dialogue. What about us? (*She sweeps her hand across the room.*) Are we just supposed to sit and listen, like in any other session? Except this time we get no break between speakers to get up and use the bathroom. (*Others in the session audience chuckle at this last comment.*)

MARY ANN: I suppose we should have told you it was OK to come and go as we're speaking.

Lights dim; spotlight is on MARY ANN.

MARY ANN (*Wiping her forehead*): I swear, they've turned the heat up in here to 90 degrees, and me in my wool dress. I guess we'll have to stick it out—too late to change rooms now.

Lights come up as spotlight fades.

MARY ANN (*To* QUESTIONER 2): At any rate…what's the question?

QUESTIONER 2: Are you saying, then, that some circumstances warrant violence, as opposed to nonviolence?

MARY ANN: What I'm saying is that sometimes being "impolitic" is essential to help stop violence. (*Looks again at the other panelists, sees* LIL *tap her watch.*) I'm sorry, but we really need to move on. (*Picks up papers and resumes reading.*) This raises the question: By what means can feminists inquire into these binary oppositions to reestablish the link between language and action as being both material in their effects and symbolic in their form? What actions can come out of our talk and what talk will spring forth from our actions? Can we, in talking about our talk about language, recast the cultural narrative so that language is understood as powerful in relation to the violence exerted within hegemonic systems of power and control and can embody choices to effect change toward that end?

We three come with impossible stories to tell. In doing so, we ask: What actions can come from language that some feminists claim is inherently hierarchical? What language can come from actions that occur within contexts of unequal sociocultural differences? We will tell different stories from those we're used to hearing about language and action, inside and beyond our classrooms. But we also want to talk about our talk as feminists. In that talking about what and how and why we talk as we do, we hope to not simply speak about but also to put into action what we mean about the possibilities for repoliticizing feminist rhetorics. We offer counterstories to those that have been used by the academy to maintain the opposition between language and action and thus reinscribe cultural narratives of violence.

MARY ANN *sits down, waving her papers in front of her face like a fan. She looks at* LIL *and* MICHELLE *for signs of similar discomfort. They show none.*

Lights dim; spotlight on MARY ANN.

MARY ANN: Perimenopause is a bitch. Hey! (*She points to a conference participant in the back row.*) She's got it, too. Look at her trying to wave that fat CCCC program as if it could stir anything up.

Lights come up as spotlight fades.

MARY ANN *steps aside and opens the door directly opposite the table as* LIL *takes her place at the podium. Broken bits of conversation enter along with smells of burned food from the hotel's kitchen.* MICHELLE *shakes her head, gestures to close the door.*

LIL: Hearing Mary Ann's opening to our session, I started thinking about the children's taunt: Sticks and stones can break my bones . . . but words can
    A: never—the cultural narrative
    or
    B: really—the new feminist trope
    hurt me.
    How do words really hurt?
We don't typically think of "stories" as hurtful words—as fighting words. In fact, in composition studies, we rarely critique the stories that people tell. There usually is no comment and response to personal narratives in *College English* or *CCC*. Yet I want to argue that many of these stories perpetuate the dominant cultural narratives, the narratives that perpetuate patriarchal culture. I see the problem most vividly in the stories we tell about teaching. These stories—these words—fall easily off the tongue, and they perpetuate the dominant stories we live by. Mike Rose's *Lives on the Boundary* received much national attention, I would argue, because it reinscribes the masculine heroic narrative—the story of the bohemian male teacher who is discovered by male teachers and who then surpasses these teachers with his wisdom by helping those whose lives are

marginal. No one seemed to ask out loud why this story is the compelling one, particularly when most literacy workers/teachers are women.

Yet women writing about their experiences as teachers haven't faired much better. In Jarratt and Worsham's *Feminism and Composition Studies: In Other Words*, Susan Jarratt chronicles her transformation from grammar enthusiast to writing teacher. During the late 1970s, she was teaching mostly Latino and Latina students in San Antonio. She writes:

> The less they learned, the more intensive and torturous became my exercises. As a teacher of grammar, I was the quintessential "subject supposed to know." . . . And since I was a straight, white person teaching mostly people of color within a social space of unquestioned heterosexuality, my teaching practice perpetuated other forms of domination as well. My introduction to the writing process and to theories of discourse through a graduate teaching practicum at the University of Texas, San Antonio, radically changed the way I taught, saw my students, and understood the whole enterprise of teaching writing. (1998, 5)

Jarratt's story makes it seem so easy. Her story is a conversion narrative: "I once was lost, but now I'm found, 'twas blind but now I see." I was once a grammarian and now I'm informed. I once had oppressive ways, but now I'm editing a postmodern feminist volume.

The conversion narrative is often found in early writing-process teaching stories. The National Writing Project seemed to perpetuate this trope: Teachers go to the project for one summer and are "born again."

What is wrong with this trope for teaching seems self-evident. Fundamentalist Christianity certainly has at its base the oppression of women and the perpetuation of patriarchal society. Jarratt's story also masks the problematic nature and the unevenness of learning any new set of concepts. We don't know why she went back to graduate school, who taught her there, what was taught, or how it was taught. This part of the story goes without saying. What does get told is the "confession" and the redemption, not the intellectual work of teaching and learning, the trying things out and failing, the change of mind that takes years—not one grad class.

QUESTIONER 3 (*Raising her hand*): Just a minute. You're criticizing Susan Jarratt for writing about changing her views as a compositionist?

Sure, she didn't tell the story in exactly the "right" ways you seem to think she should. But we only have so much time, and so many words, to ever make our point. Isn't how she told it beside the point? The main thing is that she doesn't pound grammar lessons into her students anymore. Lord knows I have enough trouble getting most of our graduate students to see that.

LIL (*Leaning forward with both hands on the podium, as if to jump out from behind it*)**:** But that *is* the point! We tend to read such narratives as transparent and thus unavailable for comment. Conversely, we read "error" as opaque, impenetrable, as if we can't understand a thing the writer is saying until it is corrected to a standard we set, one that, by the way, we don't even know for ourselves what exactly it is. Instead, we rely on "knowing it when we see it."

Lights dim; spotlight on LIL.

LIL: It's like I'm trapped in this black hole where no one can hear me. No matter how many studies have shown that teaching grammar or correcting errors have virtually no effect on student writing, teachers still "believe." But there's a flipside—the "conversion" of teachers who let grammar slide, who focus on "process" or "cognitive functions." Why not instead critique the stories we tell about teaching and writing?

I'm the incredible shrinking woman; every time I open my mouth, I get smaller.

Then again, I worry about Freire's "narration sickness." Look at their eyes glazing over. I need to move on.

Spotlight fades, then shifts to MICHELLE, *who stands for a moment, looking thoughtful, before exchanging places with* LIL.

Lights come up as spotlight fades.

MICHELLE: I'm feeling emboldened but a bit daunted by Lil's critique, especially her discussion of the conversion narrative. Having grown up in an evangelical Christian preacher's home, I find it a very familiar, comforting narrative, one that still often hooks me. As Lil suggests, the Big Conversion stories allow me to ignore and not take responsibility for the everyday experiences, conflicts, and struggles of teaching, writing, and academic work.

In general, I find conversion narratives impermeable. They tie up loose ends and answer big questions without asking them, leaving no space for dialogue. I'm hungry for narratives that are less focused on quick fixes than on processes. I want to hear about the daily choices, compromises, oppressions, and repressions. These are the stories that are whispered in the coffee houses and bars outside of the conference hotel. On my way here, I overheard a woman in the lobby telling someone she was planning to hide her pregnancy for as long as possible, so her reappointment case would not be compromised. I overheard a man on the train to the hotel talk about writing with colleagues in the sciences—how the multidisciplinary, collaborative writing process was invigorating but frowned upon in his home English department. One of my own colleagues mentioned several people who didn't make it to the conference this year because of sickness, family responsibilities, or the prohibitive cost of the airfare and hotel rooms.

The opposite of "to convert" is "to hold." Holding connotes an embodied enveloping of experience. It also implies healing more than fixing. In today's context of religious extremism, the violence of the conversion narrative becomes even more obvious as it informs body-denying, self-sacrificing, dominating (one voice, one way) behavior. In response, I move toward healing, healthy narratives, narratives that hold a number of voices. In their feminist dialogue, for example, Tuana and Cowling rewrite one of the founding conversion narratives in Western philosophy, Plato's allegory of the cave. Instead of celebrating man's ascent out of the cave into the light of the sun, they bring man in contact with his bodily basis of being within the feminine foundation of the cave. They write: "Plato turns our attention to the fire and from it to the shadow, explaining that the shadow is a sleight of hand, created by images blocking the light of the fire. But little mention is made of the wall upon which the image is cast, and in his silence we forget that the wall of the cave is as much the source of the shadow as is the fire, for the projection arises out of the interplay of the light of the fire and the material of the cave. . . . [W]e begin to feel the veiled wisdom of the cave which has been concealed from us for so long. . . . Through repetition, Plato makes us captive. Matter is always presented as a fetter to be escaped. The prisoners are shackled; matter limits their ability to perceive. The cave is a prison, the walls of the cave impeding vision of the true. The physical body is to be rejected; the senses, the emotions, obstruct the philosopher's journey to the Forms" (1994, 262). In my presentation, I want to look at the bodily effects of narratives like Plato's and to reconsider less toxic forms of storytelling.

MICHELLE's *eyes suddenly dart to the room's high ceilings and the space between the podium and the first row of chairs. She moves away from the podium to whisper to* LIL *and* MARY ANN: My voice is getting lost up there. There's too much space. Do you think there is any way we can get the audience to move up here, into a closer circle?

They both look puzzled. MARY ANN *mouths, "Keep going."* MICHELLE *smiles weakly and moves back to the podium.*

Lights dim; spotlight on MICHELLE.

MICHELLE: This is just my fourth year out of graduate school. I hope I'm not still acting like a student. Oh, my god, there's Dr. Jones! I'd better get some water. (*Pours water from the pitcher into her glass.*) Sheesh, look at my nails. (*Holds up her hand in front of her face.*) If I really cared about making a professional impression, I would have gotten a manicure. (*Catches a glimpse of her watch.*) Can't think about that now—need to focus.

Lights come up as spotlight fades.

MICHELLE *fiddles with the microphone and leans forward to continue her talk.*

MICHELLE (*To conference participants*): Sandra Cisneros opens her latest novel, *Caramelo*, with a familiar rhetorical gesture—a self-reflexive comment on the art of storytelling and its inherent deceptiveness: "I have invented what I do not know and exaggerated what I do to continue the family tradition of telling healthy lies. If, in the course of my inventing, I have inadvertently stumbled on the truth, *perdónenme*" (2002, i). (MICHELLE *adjusts the microphone.*) On the surface, Cisneros' disclaimer corroborates Mary Ann's notion that narrative can be a useful and politically powerful "mode of inquiry." But Cisneros also seems to suggest the heuristic value behind the "healthy lie." She implies that storytelling, as an inherited practice, performs along different levels of toxicity, that there is such a thing as a healthy lie and perhaps its inverse—the unhealthy truth.

QUESTIONER 2 (*Impatiently interrupts*)**:** I'm curious what this has to do with teaching.

Lights fade; spotlight on MICHELLE.

MICHELLE: Give me a break! It bugs me that so many academics have to have their thesis up front and fast—that quick fix I was talking about. The problem and solution all in two minutes. I'm that way sometimes, too, though—wanting to know in the beginning if their words are worth my time. Is it really audience friendly to map it out all at once or does it cater to a "show me the money" fast capitalist kind of reading?

Lights come up as spotlight fades.

MICHELLE (*To* QUESTIONER 2)**:** If I have trouble knowing or recognizing what is happening in my classroom, if I have trouble putting it into words and stories that make sense, then I assume some others do too. My colleagues and students tell me they do. One way to get at it is sideways, to invent, to tell a classroom tale, to create a metaphor, and then unpack it. The idea that there is a direct relationship between our stories and "reality" makes language, or words, the handmaiden to the so-called material world, or action, in a way that denies the creative effects of story and ideology and makes the "truth" a matter of finding the correct words, ones that render the classroom transparent. Cisneros writes, "After all and everything only the story is remembered, and the truth fades away like the pale blue ink on a cheap embroidery pattern." (MICHELLE *ventures a look at the audience, waits for a follow-up question, smiles at some friends in the third row, then continues.*) In her "metaphorical memoir," called *Lying*, Lauren Slater argues along the same lines, claiming that the lies we tell about ourselves can provide the groundwork, however temporary, for connection and healing. She writes, "From my mother I learned that the truth is bendable, that what you wish is every bit as real as what you are" (2000, 5). Despite the influence of her mother and her struggle with epilepsy, which severely impaired her ability to recall her life events, Slater sets off to tell a nonfiction version of her life. However, it is a version that privileges emotional as well as factual memories, and one that represents the sights and sounds of an epileptic world, where music has color and words have smells. Near the end of the memoir she suggests that she may not have actually been an epileptic: "Perhaps I've just felt fitful my whole life; perhaps I'm just using metaphor to tell my tale, a tale I know no other way of telling, a tale of my past, my mother and me, a tale of pains and humiliations and illnesses so subtle and nuanced I could never find the literal words; would it matter? Is metaphor in memoir, in life, an alternate form of honesty or simply an evasion?" (192). Although I'm not suggesting we should all start organizing our lives and pedagogies around deception, I do want us to join Cisneros and Slater in questioning the imperative of "getting the story straight," especially when it comes to narrating the vicissitudes of classroom and political experience. Like Lil, I'm interested in classroom narratives that are "response-able"—narratives that ensure others the ability to respond—more than narratives that insist on getting it all down and wrapping it up, without interruption or delay.

With this in mind, I'd like to call into question one of my more cherished and useful tales, a tale that has served as a framing device for many of my teaching experiences, including an online writing course I will describe later. This narrative—born out of my experience in feminist pedagogy—entails those pedagogical practices Mary Ann noted earlier that "sometimes support the very discourses that maintain and regulate violence as a practice of academic 'disciplining.'" This particular tale remains on file for anyone to read, as it constitutes a section of that notoriously bureaucratic document known as the "Statement of Teaching Philosophy." There, like many other applicants to the profession, I constructed an image of an enlightened, politically sensitive pedagogue.

Lights dim; spotlight on MICHELLE.

MICHELLE: Probably not a good idea to question my teaching philosophy now that I'm tenure track. Is this yet another bit of self-sabotage—what my mother keeps warning me about?

Lights come up as spotlight fades.

QUESTIONER 3 (*Standing up to speak*): Doesn't everybody do this? I mean, nobody reads the Teaching Philosophy as "true" or as an accurate portrayal of classroom life. Why are you taking it or yours so seriously?

MICHELLE (*Smiles but then answers a bit defensively*): However bogus individual teaching philosophies are, I want to highlight the effects of such a genre on our understanding of ourselves as teachers within institutions. The narratives and metaphors common to this genre inform our own classroom experiences, and the philosophy itself constitutes a secret contract between the institution and the teacher. Asking someone for a teaching philosophy assumes that s/he carries a private pedagogy around in her/his back pocket ready for any classroom situation or institutional context. I want to show how the idealized, sanitized images of teaching, perpetuated by the genre, help keep teachers in their places.

QUESTIONER 3 *doesn't appear convinced but sits down anyway.*

Lights dim; spotlight on MICHELLE.

MICHELLE: Just keep reading—maybe more analysis will satisfy her.

Lights come up as spotlight fades.

MICHELLE (*To conference participants*): The following snippet from my teaching philosophy briefly summarizes a carefully sequenced series of student-centered learning events from my 2000 Body and Technology course:

> Beginning with a technoliteracy narrative and ending with a hypermedia creative research project, students positioned themselves as both consumers and producers of science, technology, and science fiction. The categories of science and myth, machine and human, man and woman, as well as reading and writing, were . . . understood as co-constitutive, if often in conflict. In order to situate these conflicts ethically . . . I asked students to explore their willingness (or unwillingness) to assume these various positions . . . and how these (dis)identifications might inform larger cultural practices. Of course, I have to remind myself that I am not the only one in the classroom with a pedagogy. One of my primary objectives is that

students become more aware of their own philosophies of teaching and better equipped to hold them up for analysis and change.

To be sure, this classroom narrative is composed mainly by the parameters of the genre itself, with its demand for grand statement making and abstract theorizing, but it also depends upon a particularly powerful archetypal metaphor—the "good enough" teacher/mother (to appropriate Winnicott's term), a teacher who provides plenty of "safe" space for risk tasking, a nonobtrusive presence, who watches her students out of the corner of her eye as she performs her own disappearing act class after class. As Lil argues, the effects of such an imaginary figure are indeed material. The "good enough teacher" is obviously gendered feminine, the antihero heroine, who is beholden to her students' learning processes, not her own conflicting desires, for example, to be liked, to be respected, or any "narrowizing" political ideology. Act like her or invite institutional reproach. I'm not arguing that we should ignore our students' learning processes, nor am I arguing that we, as teachers, should situate our own desires and political positions front and center in the classroom. What I am arguing for are more nuanced narratives of the classroom, where we highlight those hot spots—those times when institutional, corporate, individual student, political, and teacher interests come into conflict. And granted, the teaching philosophy statement might not be the ideal place to do it.

Despite the limitations of the genre, much can be learned from a statement of teaching philosophy not just in terms of archetypal classroom narratives, but in relation to what gets left out. The "lies," or omissions, that structure the above teaching philosophy are interesting for what they exclude. Who is this teacher? What risks does *she* take in the classroom? In what ways does *she* inhabit the classroom? Although I haven't rewritten my teaching philosophy significantly since composing this talk, I did confront these questions of teacher subjectivity and ethics in a profound way when I agreed in 2001 to teach a writing course completely online. The experience put my philosophies of "the good enough teacher," "the classroom as safe space," and the more general disembodied nature of teaching and writing to the test. To my surprise, the course offered an opportunity to chart the teacher and student bodies as shifting locations within electronic writing and learning processes. What follows is a discussion of that pedagogical hot spot.

Refiguring the boundaries between the virtual and real, the human and nonhuman, the discursive and the material, forces us to move past utopian narratives regarding the disembodied teacher, the "student body" in our "brick and mortar" offline classrooms, and the virtual nature of online classrooms. In their study of women and Web imaging, Gail Hawisher and Patricia Sullivan represent Internet space as both a virtual and material microcosm of contemporary U.S. society, with all its asymmetrical power relations. Online environments, they argue, are "neither egalitarian utopias nor spaces devoid of power and influence for women" (1999, 173). The same can be said for online classrooms. Web courses do tend toward standardization (or sanitization) and often replicate commercial and institutional exploitation; at the same time, however, they can provide possibilities for its fleshy subversion. More than the traditional writing classroom, the scene of the online writing course encouraged me to grapple with the effects of a larger institutional disembodiment. I plan to elaborate on this grappling when it is my turn to speak again.

She sits down.

Lights dim; spotlight on MICHELLE.

MICHELLE: Glad that's over. Even on this friendly, collaborative panel, I still feel that old torment Hélène Cixous describes. *(She reads from notes.)* "Every woman has known the torment of getting up to speak. Her heart racing, at times entirely lost for words, ground and language slipping away—that's how daring a feat, how great a transgression it is for a woman to speak—even just open her mouth—in public" (2001, 1236). Of course, this isn't, technically, a public space. Instead, my difficulties are particular to academia. Are they also particular to this conference room and its awful acoustics, acoustics that make any intimacy or resonance between the speakers' voices and the listeners almost impossible? Perhaps my stuttering and stammering are symptoms of something much larger.

Lights come up as spotlight fades.

QUESTIONER 1: Why does it matter that institutions disembody us? Isn't this their nature? Why is it important that teachers have a sense of embodiment?

MICHELLE (*Stands up again, just long enough to say*)**:** I think Mary Ann will get at this now.

Lights dim; spotlight on MARY ANN.

MARY ANN (*Fanning herself*)**:** If you can't stand the heat. . . . One of the risks we take speaking outside conventional academic discourse—that is, the thesis-driven essay that makes its point and backs it up, that sets clear, hierarchical divisions between listeners/readers and speakers/writers, that narrates its point of view by offering an all-loose-ends-tied-up finish—is just this kind of disruption (*pointing to* Questioner 1) to the "script" of how a conference paper, a story, an argument, or a "politic" discussion is "supposed" to be read. So then, how important is it for us to finish our prepared talks—or in the classroom, our planned lessons—versus responding to listeners' questions as they come? To what extent is that even within our control? This audience is taking us at our word that we want to change the "secret contract"[1] of how we relate to them—that is, not in dichotomous "twos" but as part of a larger, interconnected whole that gives away the "secret" of a powerful collective voice.

Lights come up as spotlight fades.

MARY ANN (*To conference participants*)**:** I'm glad that you see us as inviting you to dialogue with us directly. I take that as a sign that you are experiencing your own agency in ways that the secret contract of institutional discourse—in this case, CCCC—would more often than not maintain as disembodied. For that reason, embodiment is important—to make visible what otherwise gets taken for granted as "reality," impossible to change, or at the very least, unthinkably "impolitic." Without such embodiment, it is difficult to create the necessary spaces for dialogue, debate, and discussion to occur.

Lights dim; spotlight on MARY ANN.

MARY ANN: On the other hand, maybe I should just tell them to wait until we're done! Maybe I'm being too "politic" here, as if their agency depends on my silence. But isn't that the dilemma?

Lights come up as spotlight fades.

MARY ANN (*Takes a long drink of water, emptying the glass, wipes her forehead, and resumes reading*): I like what Michelle is saying about how some feminist pedagogies—and, I would add, writing pedagogies, from Peter Elbow's "writing without teachers" to Ira's Shor's "shriveling away" of the teacher figure—reinscribe institutionalized forms of disembodiment. I want to note, however, along with Robert Yagelski in his 2006 *CCC's* essay, how important these pedagogies were some years ago as counterstories to "product" pedagogies. As Lil and Michelle have already said, it's a story that fits with cultural narratives about women as nurturers; their "dis/identifications," desires, and risks are erased in the name of the student/child. Narratives such as Michelle's highlight how much *all* pedagogies are "sanitized," that is, disembodied in a way that masks not only the messiness that Lil has described but also the violence that structures the "disciplining" of both students and faculty. And it's a narrative that both overdetermines and underdetermines the risks I take with my students in the classroom by erasing my body as what Michelle calls "a locus of meaning."

I have this hope that the violence we are forced to live with, that threatens our telling of counterstories, can be read as having a form—that is, an embodiment—and thus meaning, especially in how that violence maintains inequality and injustice. And in "rereading" these meanings, my hope is that we can then better understand the choices involved in making a self, that is, in embodiment, in the context of collective voice and action. This hope comes from spending six months in a community arts program for nonviolence. Teens from northeast Indiana, some of whom had been in a court-ordered program, volunteered to shape a performance on a subject of their choice. One experience during a movement improvisation embodies this hope. Two thick ropes were laid out in concentric circles on the studio floor at the Fort Wayne Dance Collective where we met for rehearsals each week. All of us, the young performers and adult instructors, were asked to move into the outer circle and strike a pose that represented our "outer" self—what others saw as "us." Then we would move inside the inside circle, which was much smaller, and strike a pose that represented our "true" selves. In the process of enacting and reflecting upon this improvisation, I realized that my movements took on very specific forms—a hunched back, a grasping hand, a clenched fist raised, a twisting torso—forms that I had not recognized as such. These were movements shared by everyone in the circles and even exchanged, consciously or unconsciously, as we moved. I had not, in a sense, chosen these forms of movement; they had, in this sense, chosen me. But once I understood that my movements did, indeed, have a form, I began to see other choices for how to move, including not moving at all, as did one young man, who stood outside the circle against the studio's outer wall. The cause-effect story that Lil has named had had a visible effect on how I moved in terms of being controlled by movements I had not chosen, or, conversely, being in control of how I moved. But movement, and by extension, learning, was not about this either/or: either control or be controlled. My movements changed as I became aware of how I was already moved by others and how others were moved by how I moved. David Bleich calls this a "pedagogy of exchange." Whereas before I just moved, now I could reread my movements as having a form and thus meaning. And in seeing this, I saw the forms and meanings in others' movements and thus choices for how else I might move. New movements were improvised by all. Just as jazz players exchange riffs, we exchanged movements. And meanings. We became better "readers" of movement and thus better movers.

Still, it's risky to tell stories that "read" violence as neither meaningless nor a social aberration, since telling such stories can make us individually vulnerable, as Nancy Welch notes. Such stories open us up to charges of being no better than the perpetrators of the violence directed against us:

> So here's the other challenge we face as rhetoricians: that of putting out a story, reductive and doomed though it may be, anyhow. It's risky: risky to associate ourselves with rhetoric (knee-jerk and sloganeering); risky in our postmodern, post–Cold War era especially to insist that radical rhetorics are those that stay bound to political scenes we can point to, name, and join. I've thought a lot about this risk in the past year as I've taken up slogans and chants ("Hey Bush, we know you/your daddy was a killer too"; "Hitler, Sharon, it's the same/the only difference is the name"). To be sure, these chants can be faulted by the careful academic for their "lack of nuance," yet these chants in their moment—the build-up to war in Iraq, the bulldozing of Jenin—have felt to me far from cheap. (2004)

Pauses, noting visible agitation from JANE, *the panel's respondent, who is seated in the first row. When* JANE *does not speak,* MARY ANN *continues.*

It's safer to tell a cause-effect story because it isn't seen as a story that depends upon other stories, told and not told, known and unknown, for its meaning. Instead, the story form is understood as a transparent container for the story's content or "reality," just as violence is just a "reality," an extension of our "natural" instincts and thus inevitable. This means that if violence is natural and thus meaningless, we don't have to think about how it is, in fact, learned. And we certainly don't have to consider how literacy education may be part of how it is learned. And yet I still have this hope that maybe the risks will make more sense, and that how we take them, and when, and why will be easier—maybe even safer?—if we become better readers of the forms and meanings of the violence that is so woven into the fabric of our lives.

I admit, though, that this hope is fragile. The dominant narratives of control are so powerful that sometimes I think I should stop reading the newspapers and watching TV. Here's an example from the Fort Wayne *Journal Gazette*, a synopsis of "the first insider book about the White House," by David Frum. Frum contrasts the two aides Bush has relied upon the most, Karl Rove and Karen Hughes, with Rove as "a risk-taker and intellectual . . . a reader and a questioner" and Hughes as a "mother substitute" who "loathed risk and abhorred ideas" (Gertzenzang 2003). While the verbal, intellectually driven Rove is respected by Frum, it is Hughes who seems to prevail in a White House that Frum characterizes admiringly as simultaneously "unintellectual" and enigmatically "mysterious." I take this to mean that Frum finds Bush more compelling for who he is—beyond words, in his "character"—and what he does than for what he says. At the same time Frum has come to admire Bush more for his increasingly strategic use of language to convey his "vision." This ontological power is what leaders like Bush are motivated to protect and defend, one that supposedly comes not from words but from "who one is." Keeping language as "merely" symbolic is a way to keep the ontological order intact even as those on top use language to maintain the power they have through selective use of "visionary" words.

Luis Rodriguez, in his memoir, *Always Running*, notes a similar kind of dichotomy between language and being in street gangs' enactments of violence. He sees them performing stories they've learned from the dominant culture: Words have little power. It's who you are, what you have, and what you do that determines your power and thus your ability to survive. I spent my winter break watching *The Sopranos* on video, and it's a similar story, depicting mob culture as part of, not isolated from, mainstream culture, in this case suburban New Jersey. Politicians and gang members alike thus are controlled by an unspoken ontology: who one is in the "natural" order, "beyond words." In this ontology, language is portrayed simultaneously as merely symbolic—that our identities don't depend upon it—and mythically powerful. As in the conversion narratives, a single word, if it's the right one, can change one's life.

Ultimately, to tell the counterstory to this narrative of control means risking what people like Bush want to defend: one's character in the master narrative. It means showing how powerful language, not just "the natural order," is in determining the self, and at the same time how identity is also shaped by other symbolic forms of control, such as movement. We live on the edge of this division: On one hand, we live as if words are ultimately incapable of changing anyone or anything, as G.W. Bush professes. At the same time, we live as if words are the sole means by which anything can be done; as Kristie Fleckenstein writes: "Our entire concept of literacy by definition privileges language" (1996, 916).

So I understand a little bit about why Rodriguez' gang members, as well as young people here in Fort Wayne, resist words—reading, writing, speaking them—and instead seek control through violence. If words are everything, as they often are in school, then young people are nothing because these words are not theirs. Fortunately, as they've discovered, words *are* only a small part of who they are. It's important for them to know this; they feel the domination of other people's language in their lives, language that defines not only what they say but literally how they move their bodies in space. By moving with them, I've learned a lot about the forms that control takes. And I've had to think about how this view of language and literacy as being the "whole story" in academia has shaped my identity, my sense of agency and choice, with students and colleagues, even as I seek out counterstories to help me reread these controls. I share the hope that Nancy Welch embraces as she suggests a way out of the either/or choices that violence imposes when she writes,

So while I have given some thought, and worry, to those who call me a stupid bitch and while I understand why Asian and Arab friends especially are concerned with appearing as unnoticeable as possible while flying or while crossing the border from Canada, I argue that we need to use these circumstances to look outward (and this includes outward beyond the confines of patriarchy theory) to others who also do not benefit from this new world order. What might we lose in vulnerability and what might we gain in power through becoming visible *together*? I think here, for example, of the thousands of Arab- and Muslim-Americans who turned out for the 100,000-person-strong Free Palestine rally last April in Washington D.C. despite the very real threats of detainment and deportation under the USA PATRIOT Act—a dramatic example of collective visibility. The story I've just told needs to be expanded to include this possibility of collective visibility, the needed counterweight to individual vulnerability. (2004)

QUESTIONER 2 (*Standing up*)**:** This all sounds very noble and high minded, but I am a nontenured lecturer, working my tail off teaching four classes a semester, plus directing the writing center, and it's about all I can do at the end of the day to fix my three kids dinner and figure out when I'll have time to wash my hair, let alone deal with the stack of student papers I have to comment on. If I can catch the television evening news while I'm ironing clothes, I consider that a good day. Even if I want to be *more* visible—and given the examples you've offered, I'm not sure I can personally afford to be—it's not like I have the time to devote to "the cause" when it takes everything I've got just to put food on the table.

Lights dim; spotlight on MARY ANN.

MARY ANN: One day in the department office, one of the continuing lecturers, Jessi, commented on the anti-war stickers on my office door. "You're brave," she said. Her tone was almost dismissive, as if it was unthinkable for her to make such "impolitic" displays herself. At first I thought she was implying that my tenure protected me but not her. But later I realized that she really meant it—I was "brave" because she, born and raised in Fort Wayne, Indiana, was familiar with risks that I, an outsider, might never suspect.

God, I want to take this dress off, I'm so hot. We must be right under the boiler room. Shit, my glass is empty and the only pitcher with water left is all the way on other side of the table.

Lights come up as spotlight fades.

MARY ANN (*To* QUESTIONER 2)**:** I can't tell you how to use your time or what to devote your efforts to. I can't tell you what risks to take or not take. But what I think we're trying to get at here is that when you start to understand your circumstances as part of larger systems of power and domination, when you start to connect your struggles with those of other people who may or may not be like "you," then your choices start to look different. You may find that time itself changes to accommodate those new choices. You may find, as David Wojnarowicz notes in *Close to the Knives*, comfort in seeing yourself represented in a new and public way.

I know Lil has more to say to this point. Lil?

LIL: Those master narratives, the merely symbolic, do have material consequences, particularly in the everyday lives of teachers and students. How often we forget that our everyday lives are not separate from larger systems of power and domination. I can hear so many of us saying something like, "Well, I'm just an English teacher. What does this have to do with me?" The invisibility of the teacher in our professional discourse, I want to argue, is part of this systemic violence. The more we continue to use this nameless, faceless teacher, the more we are perpetuating that violence. What concept of teacher is choosing us when we fail to situate the teacher in a classroom, at a particular time and place?

Even among theorists that I truly value, the teacher seems to remain nameless, faceless, generic. For instance, in Bruce Horner's essay, "Rethinking the 'Sociality' of Error: Teaching Editing as Negotiation," in Horner and Lu's NCTE volume, *Representing the "Other": Basic Writers and the Teaching of Basic Writing,* Horner argues forcefully about how our traditional focus on errors is part of the violence and domination of one social group over another. He argues, rightly, that errors are social and have real consequences for writers and that the research on error assumes that the social consequences lie outside the classroom rather than seeing the classroom as the site where teachers and students play out the consequences of error production and correction. Yet when Horner goes on to describe what teachers might do about teaching "grammar," he falls into the trap of the generic teacher. He says that the teacher should dramatize the negotiation of meaning with his students by having them rank and define the seriousness or significance of such different types of errors as misspellings, blurred syntax, comma splices, and omitted words. The teacher asks things like, "When does this error matter? To whom? Under what conditions?" (1999, 139–65). The teacher helps his writers see error not as a rule they must learn and abide by but as choices that must be theorized. Interestingly, he cautions teachers that this discussion, whether in a conference or a classroom, can easily become sites of domination and accommodation rather than negotiation if the teacher isn't careful.

In all of Horner's examples and cautions, the generic student is seen as the one who must be cared for by the all-powerful generic teacher. Horner acknowledges that language choices are part of historical and social circumstances, but he doesn't make the case that teachers and students in classrooms are situated and produced by history and the social conditions of various communities. Horner advocates that we teach error as negotiation. And I value that recommendation. But I also see how troubling and complicated negotiation can be when Horner's default classroom—teacher powerful, students helpless—is not the one a teacher inhabits. He cautions us that we shouldn't pretend that students do not have power to negotiate—I want to add that we shouldn't pretend as well that all teachers have the same power to negotiate (1999, 157).

In much of my teaching, I have been the one "outside" the powerful language practices of the community. When I lived in New York City, the southern, middle-class language practices I brought with me marked me as suspect. One of my students asked me one day, "And what country are you from?" When I taught high school in Celeste, Texas, my southern idiom was considered "eastern." Texans see Texas as the "South." Where does my power to negotiate come from when my students bring with them the suspicions and prejudices of the common sense? Southern English dialect = Kiss my Grits. And then what power do my students have: my students right now, southern women from the working class whose language practices mark them as "substandard"? They want to become English teachers. So how do they negotiate the power differentials when students may feel free to fill the powerful place left vacant by their customary ways of speaking—for example, "He done finished his work." Would their position as teacher be enough? To ask us to negotiate with our students means, I would argue, that we need to explain how negotiation itself is a socially constructed and politically interested relationship. Teachers and students operate within networks of power and knowledge. It isn't always the students who are powerless. It isn't always the teachers who are insiders. We need to make teachers visible in our professional writing.

Nancy Welch describes well how dominant narratives of teaching constrain us as well as what new stories might have to offer:

[S]uch a story becomes something not fully recognizable among teachers of composition and rhetoric, too unlike our dominant stories of successful teaching and learning. After all, this isn't the story of the critical warrior doing daily battle with students' false consciousness nor of the handmaiden to students' most sincere and true expressions nor of the bitch pedagogue who lays on the line what female students have to do for individual, conventional achievement. This is also not the story of the fractured, excessive postmodern feminist enthralled by the shifting slipperiness of her own selves and significations. . . . We have been, as Kristie Fleckenstein and Mary Ann argue, too exclusively, even fetishistically attached to alphabetic literacy or I would say too exclusively attached to individual rhetorical practices within just a handful of institutional situations, composition's forays into collaborative writing and extracurricular literacy scenes instigating only a partial challenge to parochial and privileged individualism. As we think about what will be necessary to tell counterstories of teaching and learning, we might consider the literacy practices and rhetorical understandings required in an age where the need for solidarity, organization, confidence and creativity with language is paramount and where the history and examples of collective argumentation and mass action are largely suppressed. (2004)

QUESTIONER 1 (*Somewhat tentatively raising his hand*)**:** I agree with you that the professional arguments about grammar instruction, both the research and the political analyses, need to be heard. We have to do a better job informing those in positions of power—the policy makers in Washington, in particular—of what is myth versus reality in our accumulated knowledge. One charge of NCTE, then, is to hire better lobbyists, to get the word out beyond the organization that we are the experts and thus should be listened to.

Lights dim; spotlight on LIL.

LIL: Here we go again; let Big Sister NCTE argue on behalf of teachers to the big guns in Washington. Michelle and I spend part of our time every year talking to our Congressional representatives about our respective National Writing Project sites. I wrangle for an audience with Liddy Dole, one of my state's senators, to argue for the writing project to continue. But I question the assumption that we just have to make our arguments "clearer" to the powers that be. These people are not moved by rational arguments, clear evidence, and well-reasoned positions. They are moved by power. When I advocate "for teachers," to what extent am I making their power less visible—to those in decision-making positions as well as to themselves?

Lights come up as spotlight fades.

LIL (*To* QUESTIONER 1)**:** My point is that I think we have made these arguments very clearly and are still not being heard. I hate to come back to another grammar example. Talking about "grammar" at CCCCs is something like talking about politics or religion at a family get-together. The debates around "students' rights to their own language, I and II" didn't reach the depths of the bloggers. Yet the intensity with which we have argued about grammar in this organization is worth noting. When we correct student writing, we often tell ourselves that we are helping the student—the one who is going to work for IBM one day. Isn't correct grammar what businesses want? Don't we want our students to succeed? It is hard to think that our circling some usage error is of the same sort of violence that is escalating in Afghanistan and Iraq. Yet I want us to see that it is part of the systemic use of violence that has been used in our society to make sure that some people succeed and others have to spend years to find the language that schools support. And there are material consequences for teachers who make visible the stratification of society and the domination of one social group that the "correction" of grammar supports, whether they work alone or together.

For instance, when I had finished graduate school, my first position was directing freshman composition as an untenured assistant professor at the University of North Carolina at Wilmington, where I first met John Clifford. I can remember one day a senior member of the English faculty told me that she didn't like this "process" orientation I was bringing to the writing program and that she was still going to find the largest, thickest red pen she could find to mark her students' papers. I knew immediately that this was a clear example of language and power domination, both to the students and to me, but I didn't know what to do about it. I can remember telling John Clifford about this encounter at lunch one day. He told me something similar to the following in reply:

In graduate school I can remember being perplexed by the negligible effect early composition research had on classroom practice. In 1929, a review of empirical studies compiled by Rollo Lyman overwhelmingly demonstrated that direct instruction in grammar did not have significant effect on students' actual writing. Needless to say this research was not acted on in the schools and colleges. But I was looking in the wrong direction. Grammar was taught not because it was effective but because it was good discipline. It was rigorous and arcane, and it privileged upper- and middle-class language conventions against those of the working class and the poor. . . . Although traditional grammar instruction functions as an almost pure ritual of control and domination, it also serves as an effective sorting mechanism for race and class discriminations, with poorer students always already speaking and writing incorrectly—a blunt reminder that school life often seems alien and hostile and offers no stairway upward for those on the wrong end of the class struggle. (1991, 47)

John and I proposed and taught a course called "Editing and Tutoring," a writing class that was to prepare those who wished to tutor in the Writing Center. Remember, John was from Brooklyn. I was from South Carolina. John had the idea of speaking directly about power and the ways that those in power wield the weapon of language against others. I went along, knowing he was right, but not knowing how to speak directly. John had our two classes become the editor for a faculty column that appeared in the local newspaper. Faculty members were invited to submit articles on their areas of research that might be of interest to the general public. Our classes, then, served as the editor, making suggestions for revision before publication. In our classrooms the tables were turned: our students had power over the faculty's language practices. They could see the problems of audience, of purpose, and the uses of grammar from the vantage point of those who had the power to name. The students had to learn how to frame their responses to these texts within competing power relations—as students and as editors—and the faculty had to learn to hear those responses within the conflict of teacher and writer. It wasn't easy. Soon some faculty asked that the classes not read their work—that only a faculty member be the editor. This conflict opened up the possibility of talk about writing that energized the campus. Yet the conflict didn't help much in John's and my relationship with the senior faculty, who voted to turn down our reappointment. The department head and the dean, to their credit, reversed that decision, but not before hauling each of us into the dean's office to let us know that as part of our next reappointment, promotion, and tenure decision, our ability to get along with senior faculty would be assessed. It wasn't easy challenging the common sense. And for me, as an untenured member of the faculty, and as a Southern woman, I was expected to comply, to be gracious, and to know my place.

QUESTIONER 1 (*Hand up more assuredly this time*)**:** This is exactly what has yet to be articulated to those in power. We're still preaching to the choir.

LIL *leans forward, ready for response.* MICHELLE *stands up, distracting* LIL *briefly.*

MICHELLE *nods affirmatively in response to* LIL's *last line, as she moves to the podium. She bends the microphone away from her mouth, and speaks to the audience.*

MICHELLE: I'm sick of this thing! I can't really see anybody, and my voice sounds all garbled. I'll just use my stage voice.

She starts speaking loudly without the microphone to conference participants.

I'd like to pick up on Lil's example about the dangers of telling or enacting counterstories, along with Mary Ann's account of embodiment and vulnerability.

Someone yells, "We can't hear you!" from toward the back of the room. MICHELLE *sighs and moves the microphone back into place.*

Mary Ann hopes to give the "violence that threatens our telling of counterstories" a form and thus meaning, while Nancy Welch alluded to the anonymity of violence, how those in control often don a cloak of privacy in order to deploy a more surveillant and thus insidious power. Faceless and invisible, the bloggers in Nancy's narrative managed to acquire even more weight and muscle.

All three accounts—Lil's, Mary Ann's, and Nancy's—remind me of Frantz Fanon's anecdote about attending a cinema in Paris, where he feels himself being seen by images of blackness and negritude. There, the power of the white gaze was in its nonlocatability, its ability to be everywhere and nowhere, mediated by what he calls "a screen of blackness, . . . a thousand details, anecdotes, stories . . . and above all historicity" (1982, 112). What does it mean to give this power, this knowledge, *a face*, especially in a virtual environment, like blogs or an online writing class that privileges the information-rich, bodiless ego? And how does one fashion the body of a female teacher in such an environment? Is it closed body, a closed mouth, a locked house? Or a warm, nurturing "presence" inside the electronic college's bloodless graphical user interface? How does one, in this context, regain the female body (or any body) and at the same time work toward (creating) the collective good? And how does one do this in a place where words are code and code is action and power?

If "rhetorical violence" is, as Sidney Sondergard claims, "the replication in language of the physical experience of pain: its causes, its consequences, its analogues in conflict and suffering, real and imagined" (2002, 16), then the unfamiliar digital rhetorics of the virtual classroom can summon for many students the painful private and cultural memories of abandonment and disenfranchisement. I would argue that this juncture of pain *can* be the perfect place to teach writing and enable the construction of a writing self. In my online writing class, for example, we discussed and critiqued the course interface, which was provided for the university by a corporation. The first assignment—the technoliteracy narrative—helped students to get their material bearings by reflecting on the ways communication technologies shape how we write, learn, and think. Many students' responses, including Bianca's below, focused on the new literacies demanded by the online classroom:

> Prior to taking this course I felt that I was fluent in my computer skills. . . . EH 372 online was quite different than my previous computer tasks. When I went home and tried to reach the [course] site my attempt was unsuccessful. A caption that read 'This version is not compatible with the USA online course' appeared on the screen. . . . Once I logged on to my course I was surprised to see the format in which the course was set up. . . . It was evident to me that my email address was more than just an address; it would become my voice for this course. . . . I based my perception of

this class on previous knowledge concerning my use of the web and in-house lectures. These closed-minded views escorted me to a bad start. . . . An online course requires more imagination and greater use of visual concepts. I found myself reading my classmates' emails to visualize who they were. . . . It was a pleasure to review the picture of the instructor on the home page. The picture gave warmth to this particular writing technology. . . . It seems that with in-house classes when there is confusion about a topic one can just verbally ask a question. With the online course I've found myself printing out my assignments that are on the site and reading them over and over.

Bianca's narrative suggests the difficulty and importance of developing an imaginary, but nonetheless "real," classroom body, including the instructor's, in an online writing environment. In this case, my classroom presence was signified partly by a digital image—a white woman's body, seated, smiling next to a computer—which, for Bianca, offered warmth to the strange course tools. That any sort of warmth was attached to such an image indicates the close connections at my former institution between the visual markers of gender and race and pedagogical proximity.

QUESTIONER 1 (*Abruptly*)**:** How so? Could you say more about those connections?

Lights dim; spotlight on MICHELLE.

MICHELLE (*Caught off guard*)**:** It's hard to talk about gender and race at my last job. It's complicated. I only experienced the tip of the iceberg.

Lights come up as spotlight fades.

MICHELLE (*Begins reluctantly*)**:** Ummm. Yes, good question. You are asking me to specify the politics of gender and race at my former institution, a university located in the Deep South. This isn't easy because to a large extent I chose to ignore the everyday experiences of white privilege and racial oppression while I lived there, so what I say here will only scratch the surface of what it's like to teach or learn in such an environment. Like many of the professors hired at the university, I wasn't from the South, but the majority of my students were. (*Hunts for a sheet of paper, finds it, and reads the following statistics.*) At the time of my employment, 1999–2002, the metro area census recorded 134,682 African Americans and 242,422 whites, but the university census recorded only 1,718 African Americans and 6,988 whites. When I taught there, only one African American professor, a woman, was employed in the College of Liberal Arts and Sciences; the university was under investigation by the EEOC for paying its Housing Department African American workers less than their white counterparts; and, due to state and federal cuts in education, tuition and fees had risen to 31 percent of the total university budget, making it even more inaccessible to low-income students, many of whom were African American.

Sets the paper aside and addresses the conference participants again.

Bianca, the student I cited earlier, identified herself in one of her posts as an African American woman, who worked full-time in addition to her schoolwork. Although I didn't explicitly identify myself as a white woman, my photo suggested I was. I assume—and that's all I can do at this point is assume—that Bianca was not surprised to see a white instructor but may have been surprised to see a female instructor in an authoritative role in the highly technical, masculinized environment of an online technical writing course. Her surprise may have produced the warmth she attributed to my presence in the course. Because I am a woman, perhaps she expected a more nurturing approach to the technology, an instructor who would provide understanding for any mistakes and confusion, someone who would make the tools more accessible and useful to all students.

At my former institution, it was very difficult for me to retain African American students in my courses, but I never bothered to ask any of them why. I remember working hard to engage African American students by including African American writers, musicians, and rhetoricians in the curriculum, but I made real connections—in the sense that we met to talk about their coursework and future academic careers during my office hours—with only two African American graduate students. I think there may have been a number of reasons for this—institutional, political, and personal. I often allowed the deferential attitude many of the students, not just African Americans, displayed toward me to create a distance between us. It was a deference learned through generations of racial, regional, and class oppression. It's difficult for me to admit that

I enjoyed the deference I received there. At first, it was a welcome relief from the open cynicism I often experienced teaching in northern urban environments. When I look back, we all used this deference as a way not to engage with each other or the issues in the texts. It was a comfortable, warm, passive pedagogy of non-conflict. That didn't happen in every class, but it was a general tendency, especially in the larger, lower-division, required courses.

And I think this comfortable, warm pedagogy was at work in the online course as well. While students did explore the influence of race, class, age, politics, corporate interests, region, and gender on their individual experiences with writing technologies, we didn't discuss how those influences might be affecting their participation in the course or their current access to technoliteracy. Most of our discussions were aimed at past community and workplace writing environments, with many students writing about lack of access to basic computer writing technologies as they were growing up.

Lights dim; spotlight on MICHELLE.

MICHELLE: That response stunk. I purposely kept the blinders on while I was at that university, and it's obvious from my talk here that my students and I missed many chances to track the effects of race, gender, and class on the course itself. (*Looks at her watch.*) It's time for me to close.

Lights come up as spotlight fades.

MICHELLE: One thing we did learn in that course, however, was the importance of creating a scene or body of conversation. Posts, and people, would go unnoticed without the structure of interchange, such as a roundtable discussion or peer-review session. While the traditional classroom allows space for students and teachers to monologue, the online classroom was built on dialogue. Monologue rendered one and one's ideas "invisible" in the development of the course. Engaging in regular exchanges on the rhetorical aspects of digital rhetoric—what forms of communication would work in one environment and not in another—we came to know each other differently, but no less intimately, than we might have in a traditional classroom.

MARY ANN (*Gets up as* MICHELLE *turns from podium.* MARY ANN *fans her face with her papers and speaks to* MICHELLE)**:** We're ten minutes over time already, and our respondent has yet to speak. I'll try to wrap this up, but I think I'm going to pass out from this heat.

MICHELLE (*Reaches across the table for water pitcher and gives it to* MARY ANN. *To* MARY ANN *and* LIL)**:** This is what I'm saying about the dilemma of wanting response but being challenged, both in soliciting it—the problem of voice—and receiving it—the problem of consequences. I think I understand now how Mary Ann's "feeling the heat." (*Waves her hand lightly, less from feeling hot than to echo* MARY ANN's *gestures.*)

MARY ANN: Nancy Welch asks, "What might we lose in vulnerability and what might we gain in power through becoming visible *together*?" (2004).

Michelle claims, "More than the traditional writing classroom, the scene of the online writing course encouraged me to grapple with the effects of a larger institutional disembodiment."

I wonder, "I've had to think about how this view of language and literacy as being the 'whole story' in academia has shaped my identity, my sense of agency and choice, with students and colleagues, even as I seek out counterstories to help me reread these controls."

Lil speculates, "If we really told the story of how we learned to teach writing and not teach traditional grammar, all of our stories would be uneven and problematic and unfinished—just as our radicalized stories would be uneven and problematic."

I want us to read our stories today as "uneven and problematic and unfinished" because that's the only way I can think of to start to become "visible together," enough, as Michelle says, to "encourag[e] me to grapple with the effects of a larger institutional disembodiment." I know that words have power—not just to "break my bones" but to heal them, too. This is the story I want to tell, however "uneven and unproblematic and unfinished." Your story, your words in my mouth, mine in yours, making ourselves visible to each other in ways we could not have imagined before. To quote Cixous, "In one another, we will never be lacking" (2001, 1536).

Conference participants *applaud politely.* QUESTIONER 3 *stands and whistles while she applauds.*

JANE, *the panel's respondent, stands up from her seat in the first row and turns to face the conference audience. Her back is to the panelists, who remain seated behind the front table.*

JANE: I share many of the panelists' concerns regarding language and its material consequences, consequences that are all too often either ignored or exaggerated. Yes, words can be as lethal as bombs. I truly believe that. I also believe that dialogue, in its proper context, in the right moment, is what we should all strive for. But I do believe that we need to draw very clear lines between what is acceptable and what is unacceptable language and discourse both within and outside of the academy. The academy is intended to be a place where discussions of ideas can take place without fear of reprisals, retribution, or sanctions. We have conventions, rules, and regulations for such discussions, encoded in student and faculty codes of conduct, in disciplinary ethics, in shared views of what constitutes professional behavior. I believe such structures help maintain a sense of civility and thus "safety," as one panelist has commented, within academe and in society at large.

Thus I take some umbrage at the implication that the classroom should be a "free" space where anyone can bring up any subject, subject others to their oppressive language and viewpoints, and basically disrupt an entire class, sometimes for the whole semester. To even cite biased political books such as *Drinking the Sea at Gaza* is, to my mind, simply unacceptable. Such books ought to be banned. Yes, they are "impolitic" and in the worst possible ways. One of the biggest problems we face right now is the lack of civility in our public discourse. Just turn on the television and you'll see across the stations news shows with individuals literally yelling at each other just to make themselves heard over their antagonists. We, as professors of the spoken and written word, should set the best example possible.

It is flat-out wrong to bring inflammatory, biased works into the classroom. Words are weapons, and students are vulnerable to the examples we set.

Silence penetrates the room. JANE *sits down again in the first row, once again facing the panelists. She crosses her legs and arms and looks past the panelists at the wall behind them.*

MARY ANN (*Standing*)**:** Um, questions or comments from the audience?

Lights dim; spotlight on MARY ANN.

MARY ANN: What really bugs me here is how Jane can, without any self-consciousness, invoke her own "impolitic" discourse to make arguments against it. Claims about the transparency of language work to her advantage—to censure books like *Drinking the Sea at Gaza* that report the material conditions of Gazans as the result of specific Israeli actions. We look away from how she makes her argument, how it ultimately supports censorship, in favor of her appeals to "civility," "safety," and "professionalism." Deborah Tannen once noted that in conversation, talking about one's talk is seen as impolite, even anxiety-producing. So for me, as the "neutral" moderator, or even as the panelist on the receiving end of the critique, to point out this contradiction, would sound petty or defensive. My "secret contract" with the profession creates these dilemmas all the time.

To what extent can I openly rebut her, an established and well-known scholar? Or should I just concede that no dialogue is possible and move on? Or how about this tried and true move—see if the audience takes the bait?

I don't know if I can last another minute in here. Shit, it is too damn hot. Maybe no one will want to talk, and we can get the hell out for coffee.

Lights come up as spotlight fades.

QUESTIONER 3's *hand shoots up.*

MARY ANN: Yes, go ahead. (*Sitting down, she notices* LIL *slumping, chin to chest, in her seat. To* LIL)**:** Lil, are you OK? Here, take some water. (*Gives* LIL *what remains in her glass.* LIL *coughs, as if waking from a dream.*)

LIL: I think I'm feeling that heat you've been talking about.

QUESTIONER 3: I like what you all are saying, but I'm not really sure how this applies to me when I go home and face my freshman composition students. I mean, I want to be dialogical as much as you do, but sometimes that's just a way to ensure that they won't listen to me or take me seriously. To them, I don't seem all that much older than they are—

although I'm older than I look—and being female and lesbian to boot in a conservative southern state, they tend to dismiss what I say without even giving it a thought. Sure, they'll listen if I tell them where a period is supposed to be placed, but if I challenge the cultural stories they live by, I might as well be talking to the wall. To them, what's ethical or moral is obvious and not open to discussion or debate.

JANE (*Stands abruptly and turns to face* QUESTIONER 3)**:** Have you tried telling them what you think about their unwillingness to engage your questions?

QUESTIONER 3 (*Taken aback*)**:** Well, I'm trying not to push my views on them . . .

JANE: You shouldn't worry so much about that. They are not delicate flowers. I think teachers worry too much about influencing students. We're *supposed* to influence them. Why else would they come if they weren't here to change?

MARY ANN (*Pointing and fanning obsessively with her paper*)**:** You have a question?

QUESTIONER 1 (*Seated next to* JANE)**:** Actually, a comment. I'd like to know why you chose to cite that particular book. I find using such books highly problematic without the proper balance of sources.

Lights dim; spotlight on MARY ANN.

MARY ANN: Talk about disrupting! I can see us already, lounging in the hotel bar, fuming over the way Jane and her cohorts have managed to twist the whole session around the issue of "impolitic" language. I can see this because in the "real" world, the world of secret contracts with the profession, with the university, with this conference, if I interrupted the "normal" talk to speak to you directly, ignoring Jane and the other conference participants, I would not be heard or believed; I'd be found guilty of being not only impolite but impolitic. The very form of "panel discussion" itself demands that we shut down, tie up, stay "focused." Jane and her fellow "disrupter" can single out one book and put us on the defensive.

In the space of this presentation, how can we possibly organize, mobilize, speak back not simply as private individuals or slogan-slinging radicals, but as teachers of writing and writer/scholars who see language as a means for change? But the seventy-five-minute conference session offers few possibilities for response. Individuals stand up and "speechify" in response to the panel, or sometimes debate or argue or affirm what another has said. But what about a collective response? Something other than those collective "moves" that already exist, invisible, "private," and simply enacted not as a choice but as "reality"? Moves such as assuming "we" academics all know and recognize what is "civil discourse," as if that concept exists in a vacuum, instead of an ongoing struggle? Or valuing the "professional" dialogue or discussion over a protest rally, such as the one taking place in the streets later this afternoon. A protest against the war that just started, conveniently televised in every elevator in this hotel. Our "professional" discussion is constrained in ways that we seem forced to choose to leave the kitchen—or the profession—if we can't "stand the heat" instead of finding out and helping members communicate among each other what is really going on, not just within our professional circles but the impact of the war and the bombing of teachers and students in countries like Iraq and Afghanistan by bombs made in the United States.

Imagination is what helps us grasp contexts and tell stories that embody the questions they raise, to offer the counterstory to that of this questioner, who simply cannot or will not imagine a context in which the book she finds so offensive might have meaning beyond hers. It takes imagination to see that the bulldozing of Palestinian homes in Gaza means that we teachers of writing and our students are both complicit in our silence but also subject to similar tactics when it comes to how power is expressed and toward what end. We are certainly not all powerful when it comes to what is said and done within the classrooms we share with our students. But neither are we helpless bystanders to the violence that shapes our words, thoughts, and actions.

I think I'm going to pass out (*Disappears under the table, putting her head between her knees*).

Lights come up as spotlight fades.

QUESTIONER 3: So then, what is the difference between imposing my views versus influencing my students? When am I enacting the same violence that has been used to keep social differences in strict order and when am I working to change that order for the better? How do I know when it's "better"?

QUESTIONER 2 *raises her hand insistently. At the same time, someone knocks on the closed door next to the panelists' table.* MARY ANN *checks her watch. But before she can respond,* JANE *interjects.*

JANE: This is a good example of how process pedagogy has undermined women teachers as authorities in the classroom. We're so busy "negotiating" power that we fail to recognize that students tend to construe us as lacking the authority and power of our male counterparts.

QUESTIONER 1 (*Raises his hand;* MARY ANN *nods for him to speak*): I think the real issue here is class. Working-class students suffer the greatest consequences in classrooms that present a menu of pseudo-choices and "free" space. They know right away the hypocrisy of teachers acting as if everyone is "equal" within the classroom—and outside.

MICHELLE, LIL, and **MARY ANN** (*Reading together, with and to each other*): In our collaborations together, we have learned how our individual voices become stronger and clearer in the discussion of shared concerns and issues. We want to share this experience with our students, not necessarily to try to imitate it but instead to extend the dialogue, to help them generate the kinds of public space we have begun to construct among ourselves.

Many of the conference participants exit the room for the next session, leaving approximately fifteen people seated in various spots across the room.

MICHELLE (*To* MARY ANN *and* LIL): Could we now have them come up closer and form a circle? (MARY ANN *and* LIL *both shake their heads.*)

LIL: We need to wrap it up.

MICHELLE *moves to the podium and speaks to the remaining conference participants.*

MICHELLE: If we were able to shape and offer a collective counterstory, it might begin with, "We teachers of writing want the freedom to engage in dialogue with our students about the material effects of words—to censor for the sake of politeness would send the beliefs, slogans, and effects underground and squelch the very writing/coming-to-terms processes that we wish to access and activate in our classrooms. To single one of us out for censure is to ignore the "we" in our dialogue. We ask you, the audience, to consider other modes of response, modes that make us all responsible for sustaining the dialogue. One of these modes is what Gestalt theorist Joseph Zinker calls "phenomenological listening" and responding (in Gorzelsky 2003, 409). Composition teacher Gwen Gorzelsky describes a first-year composition assignment intended to cultivate such listening and responding. She asked her students to respond to two of their classmates' papers, distributed without names, which addressed the 1967 race riots, by first describing their own perspective on the events then describing what shaped their perspective (2003, 414). All the students were required to share their responses according to a particular format. They had to summarize the speaker's position until both parties agreed the statement was accurate. The goal of such activity was to help students identify the rhetorical and stylistic habits that interfere with listening and fairly representing another's perspective and how these difficulties played out in the 1967 riots themselves. Gorzelsky describes her students' dialogue as "explosive and very difficult," with students perceiving others' positions out of their own grounds and interests (2003, 416). What the activity did, however, was illustrate on a sensory, emotional, and kinesthetic level the tension associated with resistance to contacting and understanding other people's positions. We ask for the same such contact and understanding here and in the classroom not for the sake of tension or conflict or even agreement but for the sake of creating the space for "creative maladjustment" to our ordinary modes and experiences of alienation and isolation.[2]

MARY ANN: If we can imagine that what we do in the classroom has consequence, that the choices we make in using our language, voices, and bodies matters, then speaking out, struggling to articulate, and then work through the choices we have as well as recognize those we do not, then we can reclaim our bodies and our work not simply as luxury but essential to our survival as human beings.

The doors both in the front and rear of the room are flung open, and others press in, some listening to the ongoing discussion between the panelists and the conference participants. Some of the newcomers are drawn into the conversation. As a group, talking, arguing, but moving forward into the hall, they exit.

Finis

Endnotes

1. See Chapter 1 for a definition of "secret contract."
2. See Chapter 1 for a definition of "creative maladjustment."

4 | Teaching for Public Space

This fourth chapter re-presents a dialogue on teaching the creation of public spaces and audiences in the writing classroom itself. We address (in no particular order) the public spaces created within the geography of the classroom, particular writing assignments and practices, and education and teacher networks, like the National Writing Project.

We have seen in our own practice how we teachers can quickly become absorbed in institutional and curricular demands and lose sight of the political and cultural geography of the classroom. We can get caught up in our institutional identities as "diligent workers," trying to fit into the program, becoming worthy of pay or promotion. And in our focus on the rigors and outcomes of particular curricular programs we easily forget the ways our everyday teaching practices reassemble or dissemble public space within the classroom. This dialogue allows us the room to reflect on these very practices. We look at how our own classrooms constitute public space or not, including everything from emotional necessities (for example, excitement of exploration and inquiry, challenge, and novelty) to political necessities (such as the freedom to self-represent and claim and act on diverse identities).

Along with the political and cultural geography of the classroom, our dialogue addresses the spaces created by particular writing assignments, such as the five-paragraph essay or the "personal essay." We situate these assignments as activities, as identity-creating, space-creating practices.

Finally, our dialogue addresses the spaces of education networks, where teachers and students come together to offer and reflect upon classroom narratives and collectively create writing curriculum for their schools and universities. Composition researcher Marilyn Cooper argues that teams of teachers, students, writing center coaches, educational software programmers, and computer lab administrators need "the autonomy and support to decide how best to teach writing in their particular situations" (2007, 226). Teachers must regularly re-create this collective autonomy in the face of ongoing privatization efforts and their attending narratives of "school failure," "official or real knowledge," and "lack of efficiency and accountability." The only solutions to the education crises, according to our national policy makers, are to hand schools and universities over to businesses (such as consultants offering nine-day training courses, textbook companies, and so on) and/or prioritize "real" knowledge (via standardized tests) over the popular and community knowledges of students and teachers. As Pamela Takayoshi and Patricia Sullivan argue, disciplinary allegiances (which are reinforced by departmental units and differential pay structure) also keep teachers "from organizing to battle common problems in their working conditions" (2007, 3). How, then, do we develop innovative, democratic public spaces inside privatizing educational policies that have narratives and logics that go against collective decision making and participation?

Our dialogue explores how community and teacher networks can resist forms of privatization and offer a venue for collective inquiry and dialogue among teachers from various (elementary, secondary, and post-secondary) professional positions and cultures. These networks can also provide the necessary tools to communicate and work across disciplines. Other networks for cross-disciplinary work include community literacy and creative arts programs, where teachers collaborate with community workers and artists to create public "thirdspaces" outside traditional school/home, school/entertainment binaries. We also hope this book itself provides another such thirdspace, where readers can join us in the dialogue and create their own teacher identities and curricula from and within their own particular personal and professional geographies.

Like the previous dialogues in this book, this one traces the "assemblages" of public space through attention to the practical artifacts of teaching (Latour 2005, 22). We hope to highlight similarities among our pedagogies but, more important, note the real and sometimes exquisitely small differences among the many ways that we create and claim public space.

> **Us:** Our dialogue in this chapter draws on jazz composition by creating thematic encounters, or as jazz musicians would say, "riffing" off one another.
> We also "rift" off of one another as well—questioning our encounters and opening up new possibilities through critical engagement.

Mary Ann: So let's get going!

Lil: I listen to NPR on my way to school and hear a "This I Believe" audio essay on the radio. "Teachers love this sort of thing," I say to myself: It seems to stand in opposition to those fake-out essays so many teachers try to teach—formula essays that children hate to write and teachers hate to read and have no function in the world. But "This I Believe," when you listen to enough of them, is a formula, too (a brief narrative to contextualize a belief, then a statement of unassailable truth). This kind of essay closes off debate—it isn't supposed to be challenged. If it is a belief, it isn't supposed to be engaged. It privatizes public space. In order to create a public space we have to question the dominant narratives—the true beliefs:

"This I question"—

Tony Iannone, a fourth-grade teacher and an active member of our Urban Teachers Writing Project group, works with his students on a "This I Question" project. His students are concerned about having to participate in the districtwide spelling bee—a yearly event that pits one child against another in the rote memorization and spelling of words. Tony's students wanted to write on their class blog, read literature, and engage in intellectual conversation—they didn't want to spend several class periods trying to outspell their classmates and then spend a half day sitting in the auditorium watching other children spell words they could care less about. At that moment, Tony knew he had a "This I Question" project. He worked with his students to figure out exactly why they didn't want to participate and to offer the district a better avenue to teach spelling.

The students had their reasons to question the spelling bee: They hated it when kids would get nervous and cry when they misspelled a word; they knew that the home-schooled kids would win anyway; and they didn't believe they learned to spell that way anyhow. Tony helped them research and explore their insights. They documented how the "pronouncer" asked one kid to spell *mare*, but with her Southern accent she pronounced it *mayor*—the student spelled the word m-a-y-o-r and was counted wrong. They investigated how they learned to spell—often by seeing the word or looking at a word evolve as they wrote it. They often knew the "feel" of how to spell a word. They also knew how to spell better when writing a story rather than spelling isolated words. So they investigated these processes and saw that the professional literature confirmed their hunches. They decided to boycott the spelling bee through an act of civil disobedience—a sit-down strike. They spoke their acts of resistance in a podcast and then met with the principal to explain their concerns with so much school time being spent on this one, ill-conceived competition.

Michelle: Inspired by Lil's story of Tony and his students, I developed my own "This I Question" assignment. I asked students in my composition course to voice their most critical questions in a three-minute audio file and script for broad(pod)cast. For two years I had assigned the "This I Believe" audio essay with some success, but Lil's story and my own desire for democratic forms and forums prompted me to take a more dialogic approach.

Audio essays, due to their sonic nature, can in themselves break down individual defenses and create dialogue. Jay Allison, the host of "This I Believe," has speculated about the particular effects of audio, claiming: "I think we are afraid of each other. I think there is something so disarming about hearing someone and hearing someone on the radio. They sneak past your defenses and you can't help but sense them as human beings. We don't have earlids, I always say. It leaves us a bit vulnerable to ambush by the emotion that's contained in another person's voice" (Allison 2001). Many of my students agreed with Allison—the audio essay, with its emotional content and voice, seemed like a more intimate form than a written essay. I hoped adding the "This I Question" prompt would make the audio essay even more disarming *and* dialogic.

Lil: *This I Question*: When my father was about my age, he went deaf—not totally deaf, but slowly deaf. We didn't even know it at first. When he would leave the dinner table before the end of the retelling of family stories or get up smack in the middle of a political debate between the left-wing children and Tate, my Republican uncle who thought Herbert Hoover was the greatest American president ever (and the most misunderstood)—when Dad would leave the table, we thought he was growing tired of listening.

I've been noticing the same silences. In class a student will say something and others around her will laugh in agreement. I ask her to repeat: "Speak up, I missed what you said."

The doctor says, "Your hearing is just fine."

My older sister, a social worker, says, "So Lil, what is it that you don't want to hear?"

I grow tired of listening, tired of listening to the same stories, over and over again.

Mary Ann: Listening is far from the passive experience that common sense suggests. Those I know who work in social services describe what they call "compassion fatigue." Their fatigue comes from listening deeply to those who have suffered the worst kinds of oppression, violence, and suppression, giving witness to these experiences with profound understanding—a form of "belief," as in "I believe what you have experienced," and "I believe your experience matters." In this kind of listening, the listener opens into the speaker's feelings, the way that sounds register not just with our minds but with our bodies, penetrating our nervous systems. Lacking "earlids," such sounds often come to inhabit our memories, unbidden, the way songs we hear sometimes replay in our minds whether or not we want them. Through listening, the speaker's experience is transformed, becomes its own kind of experience, what Peter Elbow has called, "the believing game."

This I Question: Why, then, the fatigue? Why do some listeners begin to feel burdened by all that listening? By all that believing?

Like the speakers I listen to, I, too, grow tired of not being listened to, not being believed. The energy of that listening needs somewhere to go, a way to move. Where can it go? How can I move with it, let it move me, not only emotionally but into some kind of action, to manifest that energy in a tangible way that allows me to re-present myself, know myself as part of a larger energy, a collective experience?

When I hear in others a refusal to listen, to engage, even, to believe, when this happens over and over, as if anything I or others have said was never uttered, never registered in any way, I feel fatigue. I begin to shut down. I, too, need someone to believe that what I say is true. Not to simply agree with me, but to listen deeply to the truth of my being. I find myself craving that kind of listening. It's not about agreement. It's about engagement, about being heard even if agreement does not occur.

Michelle: I was seeking a deeper engagement in my composition classroom. Besides changing the audio essay prompt, I tried to induce more collective inquiry and dialogue by dividing the students into "community programming teams." Each team represented a local community radio station and, after much deliberation, would approve the content and lineup of the team's individual audio essays. We used Boulder's community radio station, KGNU, as our model. KGNU is run solely by volunteers, who determine programming based on diversity and local interests and needs. KGNU is also a member of the Grassroots Radio Coalition, a national organization committed to "micro-broadcasting" and taking back the public airwaves. They argue, "We think it is unfortunate (and inaccurate) to call micro-broadcasting 'pirate radio' since [microbroadcasters] are not stealing anything, but simply attempting to take back some of what rightfully belongs to the public. The Telecommunications Act of 1996 might more accurately be called 'piracy'" (Durlin and Melio 2006).

In order to create a viable community programming team, students not only had to find their local, public voice but also had to develop the critical-listening skills necessary for a vibrant public space—a space where people listen deeply, even if they don't agree. Unlike much visual stimuli, the vibrational quality of sound links the participant and the observed, so much so that the voice itself can become part of the landscape, the meeting place itself. Thus, with the audio essay students can more quickly attune to moments of distance, dissonance, and resonance. For example, I'd ask students at what point they stopped listening to an audio essay or what words and phrases stuck and why. I hoped the teams and the class itself would create a milieu that valued such reflective listening.

To foster this listening, I asked students to read R. Murray Schafer's *The Soundscape*, which offers tools for identifying and analyzing various soundscapes. Schafer argues that "the general acoustic environment of society can be read as an indicator of social conditions which produce it . . ." (1994, 7). Using Schafer's heuristics, we compared the soundscapes of various radio stations and local campus environments, assessing how market forces and other institutions determine what qualifies as a viable voice or sound. For example, each programming team analyzed the Auraria campus soundscape by responding to the following prompts:

1. What does the Auraria soundscape tell us about our campus culture?
2. What voices/sounds are privileged and what voices are silenced?
3. What do the campus sounds tell us about our relationship to time and our environment?
4. What kinds of sound walls are constructed to block out unwanted sounds?
5. What kinds of relationships do the sounds, sound walls, and soundtracks (music landscapes) create?

Lil: *This I Question:* I question why personal narratives and opinion pieces in professional journals are not engaged in the same way that academic essays are engaged. I question why we don't tell personal stories in response to other personal stories or engage the stupidity of other people's opinions. I question why *English Journal* would publish an "opinion piece"—a "this I believe" piece in the November issue—by a college professor, an English educator who should have more informed beliefs. Reading her "opinion" makes me angry. I don't want to read such hogwash.

Cindy, a Writing Project teacher, sends the essay out to other teachers at our Writing Project site. Soon my inbox fills up with email messages—teachers outraged by the essay. We decide to write a response ourselves—to engage this belief. We write:

> There is a seductive "common-sense" logic to Byung In-Seo's opinion piece "Defending the Five-Paragraph Essay," which appeared in the November 2007 issue of *English Journal*. As teachers we can identify with

Byung In-Seo's panic when faced with the writing of "at-risk" students who do not fit the academic mold. We can agree with Byung In-Seo that working with such writing in the assessment age is a messy business. We even can agree that if one's goal is merely to help students pass the test, the five-paragraph essay is a way to do it. Our concern with her "opinion" is that she completely refuses to engage the last thirty years of composition theory and research, which offer students opportunities to become writers engaged in writing genres that actually appear in the world outside of school. Our concern with her "opinion," in particular, is with how Byung In-Seo insists on teaching the five-paragraph essay to "at-risk" students. (Brannon et al. 2008, 16)

And then we argue—are we being too mean to In-Seo? Shouldn't we be nicer, more measured—two teachers ask? Another two say—but aren't there uses for the five-paragraph theme for students who struggle with writing in school?

I grow tried of listening . . .

Michelle: Public space is more than agreement or disagreement. It is engagement—something difficult to create in a composition classroom where the focus is often on writing the "perfect" narrative profile or opinion piece. In my own class, what began as a highly interactive "public" writing assignment became another opportunity for students to craft an insular, challenge-proof individual essay.

When it came time for my class to begin drafting the audio essays, I used *Radio: An Illustrated Guide* and Jay Allison's website, Transom .org, as major technical resources. Although both mention the stakes and politics of radio and audio production, they mostly offer concrete guidance on creating tension and suspense, as well as tips on interviewing, recording, and editing. I asked the teams to use the texts to create their own station guides. Most of them chose the graphic novel format and composed interesting, irreverent how-to guides to making good audio. However, all of them left out any mention of community-oriented principles of public listening and deliberation. In retrospect, this might have been a good time for me to point out this omission, but I was also swept up in the technical aspects of the audio essay—teaching the recording and editing programs and making sure students were becoming adept at working with their own and others' voices.

This movement toward the technical also showed up on the rubric sheet created by the class. They wanted each other to create "a believable, emotional voice" and to insert "dramatic buttons, using powerful, direct phrases and pauses." They warned, "If you use music, use it with purpose and don't let it dominate." Also, tension and interest came up again with "Create dramatic tension—conflict then closure" and "Create a unified message and a fresh take on something." A technical aspect I kept emphasizing was a powerful opening. For the rubric sheet, I wrote, "Use the opening to create tension or interest and a strong sense of context (the more concrete and 'real the context', the better)." And finally, I added a criterion for lively, figurative language: "Be concise (carefully choose your words) and at the same time use figurative language (metaphors, images, sensory description, and dialogue) to put your audience in the scene." Along with the rubric, the recording techniques themselves also facilitated a strong identification with the individual voice and, as a result, personal ideas and opinions. Overall, a strong conflict or split erupted between the first section of the sequence, which taught deliberative, public listening, and the second section, which taught the skills of "good narrative" and "good argument." I allowed the second section to circumvent the first.

Many students produced amazing, NPR-quality audio essays, which I showcased for faculty and other students. However, I'm wondering how we might have made the *whole process* more interactive and dialogic. Composition scholar Patricia Roberts-Miller compares the sort of public sphere that manifested in my classroom to a bumper car pavilion, where students write primarily opinion pieces "that conflicted with one another . . . bouncing against each other" (2004, 49). She claims, "[The arguments] are not changed by interacting with one another; contact with one another is arbitrary (if not random), hostile, and hard on the neck" (49). Roberts-Miller further argues, "[I]f people are to disagree with one another, then there must be a public sphere where people do more than simply say their piece and then retreat to the enclave. There must be a continued interaction of people who are disagreeing with one another; an area of expression is not enough" (87).

Something else might have also helped us create a more robust public sphere: a common local issue. Bruno Latour argues that issues bring people together because issues divide them: "[W]e don't assemble because we agree, look alike, feel good, are socially compatible or wish to fuse together but because we are brought by divisive matters of concern into some neutral, isolated place in order to come to some sort of provisional makeshift (dis)agreement" (2005, 23).

Mary Ann: I hear in sonic literacy an attention to listening that feminists such as Krista Ratcliffe are also theorizing. The idea that we can't close off to sound in the same ways as we can close our eyes to visuals rings true. What also rings true is the connection between creating silences for listening and, as we three have been arguing, creating public space. There is no public space without listening. There is no listening without silence. How, then, do we go about creating these silences within ourselves and within others?

I have been working with the Three Rivers Jenbe Ensemble, a West African cultural education group for children, for five years now, teaching creative writing. I have been trying to understand how this group creates spaces for listening, for what Ray Oldenburg calls an "informal public." Latour's comment about assembling around a common issue rings true here. This group assembles because we perceive a lack in the schooling that these kids receive. However, the group does not fashion itself as merely supplemental to what schooling lacks. Instead, they are creating an alternative space that questions and re-visions the spaces of conventional schooling. In this regard, Edward Soja's theory of thirdspace provides a useful understanding of spaciality. In contrast to the traditional dialectic of thesis-antithesis-synthesis, Soja notes how thirdspace prompts "a disordering, deconstruction, and tentative reconstitution of [this] presumed totalization producing an open alternative that is both similar and strikingly different" (1996, 61). In addition, Soja states, "Thirding produces what might best be called a cumulative *trialectics* that is radically open to additional othernesses, to a continuing expansion of spatial knowledge" (61). In short, I see TRJE as assembling to create alternative spaces for their children's education, spaces that are not merely supplemental or otherwise "outside" of conventional classrooms. Instead, I see it as a place where schooling is being re-visioned by adults and children alike. It generates the "informal public" that assists in this process of inquiry.

Michelle: If we didn't have difference, we wouldn't have to assemble. Creating a common issue within the shared space of TRJE or, in terms of my classroom, an audio programming committee would allow participants to see their contradictory worries and values. The demons to a vibrant public space are the same demons that haunt grassroots community programming teams: unity, totality, transparency, and efficiency. Students would not (as they are often encouraged to do in the "neutral" classroom) leave aside their own attachments, passions, and weaknesses. Addressing a common issue within a deliberative, oppositional, messy group process would better equip students to also engage those so-called hostile audiences outside their teams.

Latour claims democracy's biggest threat is the collective political fantasy of the "transparent dome"—the dome that gives us direct access to global truths and the common good while evading the messy processes of representation and realities of diversity. Latour calls this the fantasy of fundamentalism: "[Fundamentalists] think they are safer without representation. They really believe that outside of any assembly, freed from all those cumbersome, tortuous and opaque techniques, they will see better, farther, faster and act more decisively. Inspired directly by the Good, often by their God, they despise the indirectness of representations . . ." (2005, 31).

Mary Ann: I am surprised how easily I, a scholar of language, can reduce acts of representation into simple equations. On a recent Saturday in the creative writing class, Lenny (not his real name) became a different writer. In the five years I've worked with him, it has been a struggle to get him to write anything, especially on demand. But in some moments, he is, to risk the cliché, inspired. Poetry rolls from his pencil. The previous week, he wrote a poem, "History," in response to my prompt to write about a person of the future who would be considered significant in African American history. The kids had also been working on oral presentations, assigned by Ketu, the artistic director, for Black History month. My assignment was meant to build on their research on the historical figures and events that they had been assigned. On Saturday he allowed one of his peers to read it out loud to the group, as has become our practice with drafts.

What's interesting about the responses he received was how most of them focused not on the poem itself, but on Lenny, on how the poems he has written, now and in the past, bring out a more thoughtful side, a more serious side. His peers liked seeing that in him. They did not comment directly on the poem, as I had wanted and expected, to help him get to another draft. They did not say anything about the fact that instead of creating a fictional person of the future, Lenny created a first-person speaker that we all took to be Lenny. Instead, they commented on Lenny himself as a work in progress. They wanted to know more, see more of, this other Lenny. And he obliged, writing two more poems, one about death, the other about power. Instead of going back into his first poem, he wrote two more, poems that continued to showcase this serious, thoughtful, sometimes angry, but also deliberate Lenny that his peers asked for. He worked past the time the class broke for lunch, and offered them to me to read before I left for the day.

Having Lenny write new poems instead of revising existing ones is not new in our long-term relationship. Nor is having him seek me out to read them. What was new, however, was his sense of being listened to by not just me, the encouraging writing teacher, but his peers, who saw how the writing supported aspects of his self that they liked, that they thought were important. In a sense, these new poems *were* his revision, his way of working out the opposition of writing for himself versus writing for the teacher. His peers provided a "third factor," as Nancy Welch calls it, borrowing from feminist philosopher Michelle LeDoeuff, that helped him explore the intersections between writing for self and writing for others in authority.

Lil: "Three is a holy number; don't you know that the world comes in threes?" the teacher said to me as I challenged her practice of teaching the five-paragraph theme. "Children need structure in their writing; they don't know how to write; they need some place to start."

Mary Ann: "One is the loneliest, number one is the loneliest, number one is the loneliest number that you'll ever do." What is it about numbers that is so seductive, so seemingly safe, that we read such power into them and the equations they speak through? What is it about them that sticks like an unbidden song that we cannot stop from playing in our minds? They overtake us; they insist that we listen. At times we feel helpless to their power.

The best way to respond is with another number, a different song. Stories responding to stories. You can't argue with a number, a song, or a story. You can't shut it up or shut it down. But you can count, sing, and narrate back.

Michelle: *This I Question:* Equations that I think "work." What do I mean by "work"? Every time I distribute a tried and true handout on constructing a good argument—thesis followed by strongest reason, followed by the second most strongest reason—I give my students an instructional manual for building Latour's transparent dome. I asked my current composition class the other day what they get from that kind of teaching, the kind that delivers formulas, and they answered "a rigid structure," "less responsibility," "less risk," "less potential of being betrayed by their classmates." I want to delve into this last response. It connects to what Mary Ann tells us about Lenny's experience. The response came from one of my students, whom I will call "Alyssa." Alyssa, commenting on the collaborative nature of our class policies and assignments, said that collaboration requires her to trust her classmates, and most of the time, she doesn't want to. She said the collaborative model creates dependency on others and that wasn't always good, especially when the point of school was to excel. I responded by saying something about her remark being the heart of the debate between liberal individualism and social democracy, but I'm still searching for a response that meets, truly meets, her critique. My students and I want to see better, farther, faster, and act more decisively, and sometimes buying and implementing the next new curricular reform program or resurrecting and selling the lost canons of classical rhetoric seems to help us get there. Part of me wants to please students, to help them use writing to fulfill their individual student desires and needs—whether they be capitalist or romantic—*and* another part of me wants them to question these very desires and do it in a democratic, collaborative classroom. This ambivalence, this mixed intention, came up in that audio-essay assignment and continues to come up in my work as a writing teacher.

Mary Ann: One *is* the loneliest number. Lenny had things to say that didn't exactly fit the equation of what was assigned. But to bring these out, he couldn't just write "for himself." He needed someone to listen. He found that listening in his peers. Yet he was not writing what he thought they wanted to hear. He was writing to offer them something they may not have thought of themselves, experiences with death, thoughts on leadership and power, a questioning of the historical categories and social realities that still require a "separate" African American history. He was writing his own version of the academy, a version that poetry as a genre enabled. It was a poetry full of argument but also questioning, multiplicity rather than simple either/or equations.

Michelle: Three became our number, too. Somewhere in our making of those audio essays, we began making three-minute audio enclaves around our own ideas and beliefs. Creating public space is messy and difficult—it's both individual and collective. It involves both expression and communication, both speaking and listening, and marking the process along the way. I'm reminded of a story I heard on the radio recently about a female athlete from Salida, Colorado, Diane van Deren, who won the 2008 Yukon Arctic Ultra race (*Colorado Matters* 2008). The race required her to navigate 300 miles of Canadian arctic wilderness. An amazing feat for anyone, let alone someone who had damaged the orienteering section of her brain. Because of the damage, van Deren couldn't orient herself via map or GPS. She even had trouble keeping track of time—how many days or hours she had been on the trail. In an interview with *Colorado Matters*, van Deren would often begin her answers with the athlete/hero narrative: "I did this. I had to keyhole through three days. I had everything I needed on a small sled attached to my hips. I finished the last eighty miles alone." Upon further questioning, however, van Deren told of teaming up with athletes along the way—that her success depended on it. Both of van Deren's narratives are true, but each offers a limited view into a complex event. Simple narratives about success or failure in the classroom do the same thing. They fail to orient us in the actual complex work of creating public space—the actual comings and goings, the struggles, the diversions, the fights and flights, within the process of collective dialogue.

Lil: The actual comings and goings, the struggles, the diversions, the fights and flights, within the process of collective dialogue—

We write:
    The assumption that following the rules of the five-paragraph essay will help students move on to more authentic, creative forms of writing is blatantly false. Students are taught this formula year after year, and few, if any, ever escape it. By controlling what can be said and how, the five-paragraph, five-sentence formula controls the lives and possibilities of students. The five-paragraph, five-sentence formula is always insisted

upon most urgently and most vigorously when students' languages and lives appear to need "control." In that way, teachers can absolve themselves of the responsibility for knowing how to teach writing, insist that their violent practices are in the students' interests, even get published in *English Journal*, while the effects of their practices silences students and causes students to blame themselves for their failure to comply (Brannon et al. 2008, 20).

We argue:

Lil, is *violent* too strong of a word? How are these practices *violent*? Lil, is *control* the right word? Are students really being "controlled" by these practices?

I keep hammering away at the draft, silencing the questioning. Our voice gets stronger, univocal. There is no room for dissent.

Mary Ann: *This I Question:* I still wish Lenny would go back into his existing texts, get restless and ask, as Nancy Welch would have us do, "something missing, something else?" (1997, 137) But in the context of his peers' response, I can also appreciate how Lenny's new work is, in a sense, a response to these questions. Sometimes the revision comes in the new work that represents new identifications. That is why it is so important to see writing not just as one piece at a time but also as a larger process of development, complication, dis-ease.

It still mattered to Lenny that I was listening, that I was the one who he wanted to read his new poems first. But I was not the number one in his equation of "informal public." He could write beyond the limits as he had perceived them, and his peers opened a door into a new public, one of both adolescents and adults, where he could find and cultivate his serious, mature, questioning selves.

Lil: *This I Question:* Why not quadratic equations—why five paragraphs—why three supporting examples—why does this mindlessness persist? Can't we say otherwise? Won't anyone listen?

The reviewer writes:

> The problem with your book is that these riffs and rifts overpower your aim in reaching the audience of writing teachers. You say in your introductory

chapter that you want to make a public place for college students and teachers to self-represent. However, I find your text difficult to read, less accessible, and more opaque than traditional academic arguments that truly critique issues of identity and spatial boundaries. I found your text hard to follow; I got lost when I was so frequently interrupted by other unconnected commentaries, and I could not keep up with one analysis when it was interrupted by commentary only tangentially related to the particulars of any preceding argument.

I question: Why, why is this so hard to follow? Can't you hear what we are doing? Listen up.

Mary Ann: *This I Question:* As I reread this story about Lenny, I ask myself, as Welch would have us do, Something missing, something else? (1997, 137) How is this narrative already too socially adjusted, too much part of the cultural narratives that maintain binary categories of identity, thought, and social positioning? Michelle's narrative on her sonic literacy assignment gets me restless. I hear, on one hand, the spoken word as part of a soundscape, the word as sound, as interconnected to, rather than separate from, what is "background." How one cannot close off to sound as easily as to vision, or even smell, taste, or touch. And yet how we listen is still very much enmeshed in social and cultural narratives of identification, positioning, social order. It does not surprise me, then, that Michelle's students resisted her invitation to listen and speak from a collective perspective, as part of a collective action. They have perhaps never had to listen or speak from anything other than individualized, privatized identifications and positionings, at least in academe. Whatever counterstories they may have encountered could not be heard.

So I reread my story about Lenny with these resistances in mind. In many ways, it fits the typical story of the creative writing classroom, the counterpoint to the composition classroom where creative writing's presumably free expression is subordinated to form and correctness, to the "necessity" of the equation, the holy number. Our circle of respondents, including Lenny's peers, but also several students from my service learning class, Creativity and Community, along with me, encourage Lenny's expression. Yet we don't engage his questions. We don't take up the issues he has raised. When he asks, for instance, why there has to be a separate month for African American history, asserting that it is just history like everything else, no one questions, What do you mean? No one says, It is too bad that social conditions remain such, segregation and racism remain such that this category is necessary. When he writes about death and how familiar it has become to him, how he must just get on with it, no one asks, Why do you sound so resigned? When he writes about leadership and power being about wisdom and strength, nobody says, Do you see such leadership anywhere? And are you thinking of leadership for yourself?

Instead, our responses sound more like the Cult of Personal Expression, which I recognize from many years of taking and teaching creative writing: Don't mess with what I'm saying, just tell me how to say it better. This clean separation of form and content is deeply part of how creative writing is not only taught but also how it is situated socially. For when expression is located within the uniqueness of individuals, individuals who speak for no one but themselves, it is easy to close our ears, metaphorically speaking. It is easy, then, to cast expression as something private and personal, and thus something that does not, in any final way, really penetrate us, moving us toward action or reflection. So I hear in my story how we all supported Lenny's personal expression, encouraged it, cheered him on. The easy resolution to this story is Lenny's enthusiasm to write more, bring his new offerings trustingly to the teacher/authority, who continues to praise him for "expressing himself," for his self-representation. The happily-ever-after ending is Lenny now has "found his voice."

But there's something deeply troubling about such stories. This assertion of "free expression" masks a more problematic reality, namely that such expression does not, cannot, come "freely." Instead, Lenny's poetry situates him within a struggle for identity. His expression comes not from within some deep, shadowy place within a unique self but from existing social identifications. He is already collectively identified. Part of where we failed him was to take note of this. We did not respond to how his questions in part came from Black Power arguments about race, arguments that he would hear in discussions from the one of TRJE's founders, Ketu. We did not acknowledge his collective identifications and so kept these representations private.

Lil: I begin my lecture on critical discourse analysis saying, "Norman Fairclough argues that 'Identification is a complex process. Part of its complexity arises from the fact that a distinction needs to be drawn between personal and social aspects of identity—social identity and personality.

Identity cannot be reduced to social identity, which partly means that identification is not a purely textual process, not only a matter of language. . . . People are not only pre-positioned in how they participate in social events and texts, they are also social agents who do things, create things, change things'" (2003, 160).

I then attempt to explain how language reflects both the cultural logic and "the maneuverings, negotiations, impositions, and recreations of relations of status and entitlement" (Holland et al. 1998, 13). I use as my example the statement "Clarence is just another brother" used by Angela Onwuachi-Willig in her essay on Clarence Thomas but which I remember being appropriated by a famous liberal black literary critic when he was asked by a black audience what he thought of Clarence Thomas—his reply:

"Clarence is just anotha brotha."

I continue: "So if we analyze this sentence what is happening? Who has power? How is power accrued? How is the black speaker interacting with his audience?"

The students begin thinking with me about the statement.

"The critic uses the Justice's first name, which seems significant. He doesn't say Justice Thomas, so it must mean that he knows Clarence Thomas, or is a friend of Clarence Thomas or is in some way equal to Clarence Thomas."

"But he could also be evoking this history of black men in the culture being referred to by their first name and only their first name."

"Or both. . . . Isn't he saying to his audience that Clarence Thomas is one of us, but not one of us—one of us, in that he was born a black man, Clarence, and is one of us, Clarence, but he isn't one of us—he is "other than us"—Clarence.

"What we are saying about the evocation of Clarence, we can also say about the entire utterance—Clarence is just anotha brotha—the utterance draws upon the history of black discourse—the African folktale, the double-voiced hero who could escape submission through true cunning, the African folktale enshrined within white racist culture through the Uncle Remus stories—Br'er Rabbit—the trickster.

Clarence is just another brother—like us, just like us; and he is just—anotha brother—a different brother, not like us at all.

By using critical discourse analysis we can unpack how language works to form and sustain social relations, unpack the dense interconnections between what we think of as "self" and the social practices that form the selves we understand, or the possible selves we "author" through the various identities we practice. In order to act in the world, we must take up some positioning; we must author ourselves. In this instance of the black critic, he draws upon the heteroglossia, the voices that constitute his and his audience's history and his understanding of these worlds in order to give shape and meaning to his thoughts on Clarence Thomas as well as to operate within the larger social world in which he is functioning—the competing worlds of critic, male, black, speaker, listener—the actual comings and goings, the struggles, the diversions, the fights and flights, within the process of collective dialogue.

I wonder to myself, "Does anyone understand what I'm saying? Is anyone hearing me?"

Mary Ann: Michelle's discussion about our fantasies of democracy, of Latour's "transparent dome," gets me restless yet again about how I have told my story about the TRJE session and Lenny's development as a writer. Like Lil, I want to question my beliefs, and I want to encourage my students to do likewise. Yet I'm seeing that in the questioning that I'm doing, it's my own narratives that are beginning to yield their "messiness," what Michelle calls "the messy processes of representation and realities of diversity"—the actual comings and goings, the struggles, the diversions, the fights and flights, within the process of collective dialogue. Lil comments on "three" as a holy number, leading me to question the "third factor" as I have represented it here. And also to question our own "three"—the three of us, writing all these years together. There is no magic equation, no holy number, I concede. But I do find certain analytical approaches, certain theories helpful. Perhaps it is not a matter of just critiquing the limitations of structures but revisioning them. This leads me to question the multiple positions, the "assembly" of voices and viewpoints that my narrative discloses, that I have yet to fully explore and engage, as Michelle is doing.

I also think of Holland et al.'s book, *Identity and Agency in Cultural Worlds*, in terms of the tensions these authors identify between cultural and constructivist views of identity and agency. Their argument is that neither cultural nor constructivist views adequately describe the potential for individual agency within the collective realm. This makes me question the story I have told about Lenny and the other TRJE kids in the writing group. In the first version it's as if I've written myself out of the equation except as a supportive, listening presence. In the second version,

I've written Lenny and the other kids out—they are uncritically listening and supporting, and I'm questioning that, as well as questioning my own listening and supporting. Both versions make it far too easy to not engage listening nor to engage silence. Yes, I want to question listening, but not whether it should be part of what we do as writers and teachers. I do want to "disorder, deconstruct, and tentatively reconstitute" what listening is. Similarly, I want to question form, just as Lil and her colleagues are questioning the five-paragraph theme. But it doesn't mean I don't want form or analysis. It does mean it needs to be revisioned.

From here I return to my narratives, reflections, and analyses and go back to listening. What have I suppressed or excluded that might tell me more about what's going on in our writing group? Where am I overlooking the "messiness" of difference in favor of the "transparent dome" of my fantasies of democracy and public space? There is, of course, more to the story of TRJE as a collective entity that I need to tell. The problem is, of course, that nothing ever says it all. Stories always leave something out. Arguments suppress other viewpoints. But as Lil says, isn't there a way to engage this?

So I return again to our responses to Lenny, and I remember how, when he first read his "History" poem, we did in fact, ask him what he meant about the problem of having a separate history for African Americans. Lenny told us how history shouldn't have to be separated in this way, that he didn't agree with this separation. History was history. No doubt part of Lenny's answer is informed by his biracial identity. But I was not thinking about that when I gave the assignment to write about a person significant to African American history. At that point, one of the other kids, Sharon, asked if that person had to be significant to blacks only. I instantly felt a lot riding on my response; I could not deny the significance of African American achievement as something different than individual heroism. And yet I had to see that achievement in broader terms, for the greater good, not just one group separate from another.

This I Question: In the questioning, I "re—member" (as Ann Berthoff exhorts us to do). I remember not just the support, encouragement, and belief of our work within TRJE. I remember the issues and the questions. I remember how much our answers mattered. I remember listening. I remember the silence that surrounded us as the answers drifted away and we were left with each other, re-presented anew.

5 | Endings in Beginnings

The Borderlands of Public Space

Making thinking visible, working against genre expectations, feeling the limits of words and form—we find ourselves bordering on the incoherent in an attempt to forge a new coherence, a new public space. But right now, as we face the final pages of this book, it feels, well, scary to be here—almost alone and adrift at sea.

We want to speak back, speak back to English departments, to universities, to a culture that separates teachers from each other and students from their words.

We want to speak up for those of us who teach writing.

We want to speak back, speak back like Min-Zhan Lu did when she questioned the interview-with-the-great-theorist feature that *JAC* has done for many years. Min-Zhan Lu critiques Andrea Lunsford's interview with the writer Gloria Anzaldua in a special issue concerned with postcolonial studies. Anzaldua's interview, like most of the other writer/theorists' interviews, reveals that she knows very little, if anything at all, about the work of composition studies, yet she feels perfectly confident in speaking to composition scholars. Min-Zhan Lu's concern in this essay is to make visible—as the title of her essay indicates—"the vitality of the ungrateful receiver." She speaks back to postcolonial studies about what composition

offers it, rather than always being the one receiving the gifts of "theory."
The irony, though, is those reading Min-Zhan Lu's piece, and those who
may be reading these words, are, more than likely, the ones already taking
notice of composition's contributions. And while Min-Zhan Lu certainly
documents how knowledge in our field contributes to a richer understanding of theory, the theoretical and pedagogical advances she points to
escape notice by those in other areas of English studies.

So we who teach writing remain closed off from public space.

The asymmetrical relations within English departments are just a
piece of the problem. Even the theorists who we might call on, the theorists who should know better, the critical educators, whose work like
postcolonial theory has enriched our own, don't understand and don't
listen to teachers of writing. Henry Giroux, Peter McLaren, and Stanley Aronowitz, among others, have helpfully critiqued Marx's distrust
of education as a site of cultural transformation. The distinction these
theorists make between schooling—Marx's view of education as social
control—and true education—the potential to transform society where
the learner is an active subject, committed to self- and social empower-
ment, has animated the radical social project of teaching writing. Yet how
writing instruction is figured in the work of critical educators is highly
problematic, and it is never seen as part of educational transformation.

Rather, teaching writing (composition) is viewed as mere "training"
—in which students acquire skills that will be directly translated into
better job performance in college and beyond and where the learner
is subjected to the transmission of knowledge—"banking education,"
standardization, and control. Aronowitz and Giroux in *Education Under Siege* put it this way: They understand the proliferation of writing
programs and the writing requirement in the first year of college as part
of the exclusion of the liberal arts from the lower levels of the college
curriculum. "The subordination of literature and history to 'skills acquisition' . . . " [they argue, is part of] the "gallop towards the removal of
. . . elements of critical thinking that [are] inscribed in the traditional
curricula" (1987, 62–63).

See, these guys don't believe we think. They see our work as part of
the problem.

Arnowitz and Giroux *do* see a space for "the autobiographical mode
of inquiry." Autobiography for them "is a way to help students discover
their own relation to school and to language. [Students] may see the ways

in which the texts of everyday life such as family, peer relations and mass culture are not merely activities or institutions 'out there' but become fragments of that praxis by which we form ourselves" (65).

Would they see the stories we want to tell today in this "mode"? Like this one:

> **LIL:** At dinner the conversation, like many family dinnertime conversations, turned to religion. Religion was the last thing I wanted to argue about. But her voice was calm, not pompous in that haughty sort of way, and she didn't give that litany of things she would, or had, or was going to give up for Lent—but instead she spoke of what she was going to do for Lent. What she was going to do, what she was going to do for forty days, what she was going to do in those quiet moments of prayer and thought and reflection—was try to love her mother, or forgive her, or just try to understand her once, unaccompanied by pain, or agony, or shame. For once, I wanted to listen to this religion, to take it in, deep into my soul, to linger there, to imagine a dinner conversation that for once was not the last thing I wanted to argue about, but to feel, to sustain, to linger in this moment of forgiving.

We wonder if they read Dorothy Holland and her colleagues, whose research on identity formation and language illustrates the partiality of both the social and cultural standpoints on identity. "Identities," they argue, "are improvised—in the flow of activity within specific social situations—from the cultural resources at hand. Thus persons and, to a lesser extent, groups are caught in the tensions between past histories that have settled in them and the present discourses and images that attract them or somehow impinge upon them. In this continuous self-fashioning, identities are hard-won standpoints that, however dependent upon social support and however vulnerable to change, make at least a modicum of self-direction possible. They are possibilities for mediating agency" (1998, 4).

The problem for us teachers is that this practice of autobiographical inquiry—what we are doing here in telling our stories—and that we do in writing classrooms everywhere—is that these critical educators don't see it as part of writing instruction. Rather they associate autobiographical inquiry with radical educational practices in countries like Nicaragua where the objectives of democracy for whole populations are paramount.

In contrast, writing instruction in the United States is part of conservative, standards-oriented, oppressive education.

We know that composition/writing instruction can easily be seen as guilty of the skills and standards and job preparation instrumentalism of which it is accused. The textbook industry is dominated by handbooks of usage, rhetorics of argument, and the research paper. You know—the "skills" that students need on their jobs, at the university, and in the workforce. Some of composition's most radical scholars have written textbooks of this ilk—sold out, as it were—to the capitalist project.

Richard Miller, in an essay in *College English*, "The Arts of Complicity: Pragmatism and the Culture of Schooling," explores why those who teach writing are often taken by Freirian critical arguments. He says, in part, that Freire appeals to marginalized writing faculty because he gives them a rationale of working for social justice that makes the acceptance of their lowly status more palatable. He argues that connecting our work with Freire's "is just another story we tell ourselves about literacy work, a way to make it semester to semester that preserves the teacher's sense of self-esteem" in the face of overwork, little pay, and no respect (1998, 15). It gives us a way to say to ourselves that we, unlike our colleagues in literature and history, are doing something important—developing critical citizens, when all the while, the best that we do is help students become better bureaucrats—better cogs in the corporate machine.

So is *that* what we are doing?

Miller is allowed to make this claim, just as theorists of all stripes are allowed to ignore our work, because their claims about writing and writing instructors tap into the common sense—the stories the culture tells itself about the need for "basic skills." Teachers of writing have always had to contend with these stories, unlike other disciplines, and are often contained by the arguments and practices that come from them: demands for empirical standards of proof of our effectiveness; large numbers of beginning teachers, many of whom, if they had a choice, would not be teaching writing at all; enormous workloads, little pay. We seldom get to name and enact our own programs; indeed, writing requirements are often there because of these functionalist values. If what calls us into being is the very conceptual understandings that our best professional knowledge refutes, we exist in treacherous territory from inception.

The complexity and problems of composition as a field makes those of us who teach writing feel that our words must/do/inevitably reinscribe the "banking" model of education. It feels as though we are powerless, with our only option being assimilation.

To claim agency through the creation of public space, we return to the theories and theorists who have helped us find another way, not only to resist, reject, and critique this common-sense narrative, but to imagine, and even enact alternatives: Soja's Thirdspace, Welch's getting restless and revisioning binaries, Holland et al.'s improvising identities. We return to them here, now, in stopping the entailment of our logic, to reclaim the power of our words.

In academic writing, we are supposed to stick to the point, stay focused and on task. Right? Yet this book, coming at a time of deepening economic crisis in this country and the world, finds us feeling, in some ways, very far away from the conversations we've had and are still having about writing instruction. We come back to Nancy Welch's call for revision as a practice of "getting restless." In doing so it feels like we've drifted far, far away. The tide sweeps us back to those voices that say, "We need jobs! We need resources! We need money! We need to survive! How can we make this happen?" People close to us are in peril. At times, in the safety of tenure, we, too, feel the ground shifting: Reuse those paper clips, take unpaid furloughs or pay cuts, teach larger classes, do more with less. We are bombarded with the continual social drumbeat to face *reality*, which is a reality that assumes that the banking industry as a capitalist enterprise cannot be altered. We are stuck with this economic model. We have to pay off the very people who caused this system to crash.

In composition, we hear a similar drumbeat: that the banking model of education cannot, in any fundamental way, be altered, and that (according to Miller) the stories we tell are just like religion was (he assumes) to Marx.

Does that make us Holy Rollers in the church of Paulo Freire?

MARY ANN: Here's another story:

Tom and his wife, Becky, (not their real names) were union auto workers for almost a decade and a half. Tom's father and grandfather had also been UAW workers. They have four children and, more recently, a grandchild. The union had ensured they would earn a living wage with good benefits. The work, throwing steel, as he puts is, was hard but rewarding in that it provided the basis for home, family, and community.

Tom and Becky were pink-slipped two years ago on Christmas Eve. The union secured them money to return to school and earn degrees that would presumably provide them with the skills to enter new, twenty-first-century jobs. Tom, who had finished a bachelor's in English with a concentration in writing, started the MA in English. Becky began a degree in accounting. They put their beloved rural house and acreage on the market to help make ends meet.

Then last year the bottom fell out of the economy. They took their house off the market and tried yet again to make every penny count. And this year, their money from the union's hard-won concessions runs out when they graduate this May.

Tom's thesis, a multigenre book of poetry, short stories, letters to the editor, memoir, and other "borderlands" genres both describes and enacts his "restless" (as Welch might describe it) movements between the world of school and of home and job. He describes these worlds as opposite banks of a river that runs through his life. For Tom, poetry is what connects these worlds that otherwise would remain not only opposite but deeply conflicted.

Tom began with the image of language as a bridge. But try as he may, the bridge did not work; the shifts in genre, tone, voice, and subject did not smoothly run together as he had hoped. The fragments of language stayed just that—fragments, the movements among and between them seemingly random and chaotic, "drifting."

He was doing what he was taught to do—take risks, mix up forms, embrace the contraries. The river was his borderlands, but he was clearly drowning.

Here you, my reader, are probably getting caught up in Tom's struggle: First his job, now his thesis! Probably the last thing you want me to do is drift away from that struggle and return to theory. But I need to drift, to get restless, and ask, as Nancy Welch would have us ask, "Something else, something missing?" in this story? Otherwise, it sounds like I am preparing you for either triumph—Tom bridges the two worlds and lives happily ever after—or failure—Tom drowns in the struggle to reconcile them. That's not the story I want to tell.

But here's what makes it so hard to tell any other story:

Let's consider for a moment what Richard Miller and others are assuming about our "belief" in Freire, and in the dialectical relationship between belief and questioning, action and reflection. Let's start with the assumption that our "religion," the beliefs that inform our actions—in this case that Tom's thesis, as well as his Master's in English, might actually matter to the rest of his life—are merely "the opiate of the people," in this case, writing teachers. If, as Miller suggests, the contingent faculty who by and large teach writing in the university are turning to Freire as an opiate for solace against a reality written in stone, then belief—in values, relationships, and ways of being—are unable to effect any change in the material conditions that create the need for solace in the first place. However, as Phil Gaspar explains, Marx's comparison of religion to a painkiller "is only partly right": "Ruling elites have used religion to mobilize people for their own purposes. On the other hand, religion has often played a central role in movements of the poor and oppressed fighting for social justice, the U.S. civil rights movements of the 1950s and 1960s being just one example" (2009, 14). Religion, Gaspar argues, is not the enemy; instead it is "like other parts of a society's ideological superstructure . . . the product of underlying material realities" (14). It is not a disease but rather a symptom of injustice and inequality, one that can just as easily mobilize people to action as it can offer solace for those conditions.

Back to Tom:

If language, and in particular, poetry, is supposed to be the "glue" that holds disparate worlds together, then why wasn't it working? Why was Tom struggling to build that bridge? Did Tom somehow miss out on learning the foundational skills necessary for verbal bridge building? Did he, instead, squander his time on poetic opiates that caused him to drift away from the job at hand, namely making a living wage? Who was he to be writing poetry in an economy like this, anyway? This was a question Tom had asked himself more than once.

Maybe, as Miller suggests, poetry is another story that keeps Tom from facing the harsher realities of his life, namely that there is no bridge that can possibly save him. The economic waters are too high and swift; nothing can be built in the face of such conditions. Maybe the best we can do is use stories like Freire's to keep us going, even though we know we can do nothing about that river. Rivers, after all, are beyond anyone's control. When they flood, they flood. No use arguing about that.

Who was he to be writing poetry at all?

Yes, poetry, like religion, can be used for solace against injustice and equality. It can help us "keep the faith" that our lives matter, that survival is important. But sometimes some stories would have us believe that some lives are more important than others.

But what of poetry's other potential: for mobilizing us to action? Where is Tom's story headed if not for just another feel-good moment? Another opiated drift away from hard, cold reality?

Tom and I discussed the first completed draft of his thesis. I'm stuck on the West Bank, the one Tom identifies as school, watching him drown. He has to finish in May because the money is gone then. He has to finish; there is nothing else he can do.

"I'm not sure I see the bridge," I said, grasping for what to say. Was this the cold, hard reality Tom was supposed to face?

Tom listened, as he always has. We've known each other for the nine years he's taken classes, first as an undergraduate and now as a master's student. I've always admired Tom's work ethic. Even while he and his wife were working full-time and raising their children, he always found time to write. My efforts were considerably more sporadic, and I have no children and I throw my fingers across a keyboard, not steel on a factory floor. Tom is as steady as they come.

"I think it's about being able to speak from within the struggle to move back and forth between the two banks," Tom replied. "It's the river that shapes the two banks. It has the power to shape its own course."

I thought of getting restless, about the river as a borderland where identities could be revisioned and alternative actions imagined. But the borderlands are often dangerous places. Who was I to suggest Tom write from there? The river was already high; he could be swept away.

"Yes," I agreed. "It's the river. A bridge would put you over it. But what if you wrote through it?" There, I said it. I'm following what my Holy Trinity of theorists have guided me toward—thirdspace, borderlands, sites of excess, of what lies beyond the social mirrors we gaze into for our sense of identity.

I continued fumbling for what to say. "What if you made this more dialogical and also dialectical? The voices don't seem engaged; they are just fragments drifting apart." Drift, I remind myself, is—like religion, like poetry—a symptom, not a cause, of injustice and inequality. Then for some reason I blurted out, "I wish we could collaborate and write this together." I said this not because I wanted to bail Tom out (as if I could) or for some celebratory reason that so-called expressivists have been accused of, or take over his writing. I said it because I, too, wanted to move from the West Bank, from the banking model of education, where I was finding myself stuck and without any good options. I wanted to question the idea of the "invisible" teacher, the writer who creates in splendid isolation outside of conversations, outside of her actions in the social world. But we were, after all, "doing school," and a master's thesis is supposed to be a solitary work of scholarship.

Tom, as was typical, seized on what I had floated as a somewhat frivolous, even wistful idea. "Why not?" he asked. He had already revisioned the whole "one and only" notion of thesis directing by making my husband, another of his professors, and me co-directors rather than giving way to the built-in hierarchy. No wonder his wife adores him!

And then I had to think, Why not? Why couldn't we collaborate?

"Time," I said. The words were so rehearsed I could barely feel them any more. "I'm so pressed I can barely keep up with what I'm already doing."

Tom, again, listened. But his silence told me he still wanted to do it. It was up to me. Would I move from the West Bank and meet him in the river?

Talk about drifting—I was supposed to write this paper about collective identities and the community arts organization I've been collaborating with for the past six years. It was in large part my work with the Three Rivers Jenbe Ensemble, or TRJE, that informed my conversation with Tom. I had learned from them much about the value of language, not to build bridges over roiling waters but to value and work through its excesses. I recognize my own, impulsive invitation to Tom as rooted in the power of collective action that TRJE demonstrated in making a difference in the lives of the children, parents, and audiences who gathered to participate in West Afrikan drumming, dance, and cultural education. Poetry and the arts do offer solace, but they can also mobilize us to action. I could not stay on the West Bank and watch Tom drown, or simply call out advice; I had to act—without taking over, without "saving" Tom, without authority.

Tom emailed me about his thoughts toward revision, then I emailed him back about ways he might think about his draft, and we went back and forth a couple of times. When he showed me his next draft, our emails were part of the book. When I read them, I felt relief. Now I understood what his book, his experiments in language, were both saying and doing. Now I understood my own stake in his work. He called out, and I responded. One thing I had learned from

TRJE was the centrality of call and response in African and African American culture. I had only seen myself as doing the calling.

What "skills" did Tom learn from writing a "creative" thesis? Were they bankable, as Miller would have us believe we have no choice in teaching? If anything, I would say Tom has learned, as I have, a valuable skill in how to turn toward, not away from, the excesses of language and meaning in which we are all adrift. He reached for an identity that included both banks but was also Other. When do a thesis adviser's words actually appear in a student's text named as such? The faculty member's words/ideas appear all the time, but always surreptitiously, privately. Here's where Tom created public space, by claiming what has been happening under the deep flow of our collaboration and making it visible. In doing so, it changes the nature of our social relations. Solace? Yes. But also social change? I think so.

MICHELLE: What difference does it make that we write and teach writing? How can we address this question, individually and collectively, so as not to simply critique the profession or offer hope but to shift the framework that makes this the question in the first place?

What difference does it make that we write and teach writing? For important workplace skills? Just like religion, there's nothing inherently wrong with workplace skills or teaching them. It's how workplace skills get used, like religion, by the ruling elites to advance their own interests, that concerns me. *The Job Training Charade* by Gordon Lafer argues that businesses and politicians keep arguing for more workplace education, such as technical writing, when that's really not what is needed. The argument that the current workforce doesn't have the necessary skills for the twenty-first century is a smokescreen for the continued drop in wages and the continued drop in the need for skilled labor (as companies go overseas). So if we are teaching "writing skills," what or who are they for? Does the "banking model" of literacy education allow for the fact that many of our graduates will be working in customer service jobs, where the most important skills are cooperation and a pleasant disposition? The Bureau of Labor Statistics this year reported that the health care, biosciences, and technology industries will create the most new jobs this year. However, customer service and sales associate jobs will continue to dominate the job lists. With systems analysts and actuaries also heading the lists, it's unclear where writing skills are really that useful in the workplace, although employers and politicians will continue to use lack of writing and math skills as excuses for the loss of jobs and lower wages.

Most of us do teach writing skills but hopefully in the context of practice or praxis—reflective action. For the last two semesters, I've helped my students develop writing skills within a critical-rhetorical praxis focused on public discourse and the struggles over public space. They assess written texts, alongside gestures, spoken words, and visual images—all artifacts that arise in relation to one another from the scene of conflict—and create their own public discourses and audiences. Last semester students and I focused on one particular conflict over public space—the DNC, which took place on our campus. School was dismissed as our campus administrators rented the spaces to the Secret Service and Comedy Central, one of which became the notorious "Freedom Cage," where protestors were sequestered behind cement barricades and barbed wire. Given this situation, I asked students to take original photographs of some aspect of the DNC and report on it in terms of public versus private space. However, the public/private binary I set up quickly became a useless framework as students came back with photographs of themselves and their friends working sixteen-hour bartending shifts at downtown restaurants (one of which had been literally taken over by CNN), photographs of friends being arrested during various protests, and photographs of Barack Obama, or what could have been Barack Obama, from a block away. Public space? Private space?

My own investigative reporting took me into several thirdspaces—spaces between traditional private and public boundaries. Edward Soja argues for the use of thirdspaces to open up our thinking about traditional binarisms: "I try to open up our spatial imaginaries to ways of thinking and acting politically that respond to all binarisms, to any attempt to confine thought and political action to only two alternatives, by interjecting an Other set of choices. In this critical thirding, the original binary choice is not dismissed entirely but is subjected to a creative process of restructuring that draws selectively and strategically from the two opposing categories to open new alternatives" (1996, 6).

The first thirdspace, which challenged my assumptions about public/private boundaries, was the U.S. Mint Protest, planned by a coalition of direct action protest groups called Recreate '68. Recreate '68 had already received plenty of local press as the "bad protestors"—anarchists who were there simply to cause trouble. (The mainstream press, when it does cover protestors, likes to divide them into good and bad categories.) As I found my place in a circle around the Mint, I was surrounded by mostly young, white people dressed in fairy costumes tossing paper coins and chanting together for the Mint to levitate and redistribute the wealth. (Which reminds me of Bernacke's lastest chant, "2010 will be a year of recovery," "2010 will be a year of recovery.") Even the Yippie Pie Man was there, yelling, "Don't be a spectator, join in the spectacle."

When I heard the Yippie Pie Man's words, I had one of those moments Janice Lauer would call "a moment of severe cognitive dissonance." With demonstrators on one side and reporters on another, I had a difficult time figuring out who the spectators really were, who was filming whom, who was on the inside and who was on the outside, who was "press" and who wasn't. As reporters approached demonstrators only to be met with more cameras, and as demonstrators became citizen journalists, posting their videos and news on local mainstream and alternative media sites, both groups challenged the lines between private and public media, and both created, taken together, a diverse public narrative of the DNC. The media gaze was redirected from top-down political coverage toward neighbors and one another. My binary was breaking down big time. And the Yippie Pie Man's slogan, appropriated from the original '68 protest was interrupted by new forms of citizen journalism.

That's not to say some private spaces were not heavily policed. An ABC reporter was arrested (by a deputized security guard) for trying to film people walking out of one of the big private parties, and my favorite convention video is still the footage of *Democracy Now!* reporter Amy Goodman going from convention suite to convention suite trying to get into various corporate parties. (There were 1,200 corporate parties, considered "delegate training," at last year's DNC.) The "bouncers" she encountered were huge, but each looked like he had seen a ghost. So it's not that there wasn't an inside or an outside; it's just that some of those marginal inside boundaries were eroding. Microjournalism is now a primary means of protest and communication for groups, like I-witness and Glass Beads Collective, and ironically, the growing number of people engaging in microjournalism has been used as evidence against truly accessible free-speech protest zones. When the Bl(a)ck Tea Society sued Boston in 2004 for a protest space "within sight and sound of the intended audience," a federal judge ruled, "[W]e think that the appellants' argument greatly underestimates the nature of modern communications. At a high profile event, such as the convention, messages expressed beyond the firsthand sight and sound of the delegates nonetheless has the propensity to reach the delegates through television, radio, the press, the Internet and other outlets" (in King 2007).

As Holland et al. argue, "[I]dentities are improvised" (1998, 4). They further explain this continuous process of improvisation: "In our view, improvisations, from a cultural base and in response to the subject positions offered in situ, are, when taken up as symbol, potential beginnings of an altered subjectivity, an altered identity. Such productions, we believe, are always being appropriated by people as heuristic means to guide, authorize, legitimate, and encourage their own and others' behavior. As an often unintended but sometimes purposive consequence, there is a continuous process of heuristic development: individuals and groups are always (re)forming themselves as persons and collectives through cultural materials created in the immediate and the more distant past. In this process of heuristic development, culture and subject position are joined in the production of cultural resources that are then subjectively taken up" (18).

I saw how these new citizen journalist identities appropriated the accoutrements of the mainstream press (press passes, seats in the big media tent, and published news blogs) and improvised new on-the-ground (sometimes literally) reporting. While the cameras ostensibly served to record police brutality, they were also recording the recording—that is, the movements of the mainstream and alternative press, and at the RNC, the harassment and mass arrests of journalists from across the political spectrum, including Fox News.

Back at the U.S. Mint Protest, I noticed the swarms of cameras shift toward a smallish woman off to the left. It turned out to be Michelle Malkin, a conservative blogger who was taking her own pictures (in support of her various conspiracy theories no doubt). When Malkin was called out by conspiracy theorist, Alex Jones, lenses clashed, and the scheduled protest became a battle of footage. I noticed several of the protestors trying to "jam" the media storm by yelling into the cameras but to no avail. Before long Secret Service agents, teeming out of unmarked white vans, asked people to disperse, and everyone did—somewhat lazily but thoroughly. I stood for a while on the corner of 15th and Cleveland, watching everyone tuck their cameras back into their pockets and head to their various meeting places. Approximately two hours later, police would back protestors into that very corner and detain them for ninety minutes, many of them journalists and quite a few of them individuals collecting photos to post on Flickr.

One of them was a student in my friend's class at the Colorado Film School. Professor Geoffrey Chadwick's student film crews were "embedded," press passes and all, on the convention floor and in the various marches and protests. Chadwick was supervising 110 students and faculty members during his week off and had just taken on sixteen sections of film to pay the bills. He certainly would have benefitted from any action toward wealth redistribution. Press credentials did not protect Chadwick's student, who was arrested during the police sweep. Although the ACLU declared the arrest and many like it illegal, the student himself was thrilled with the footage he got in "Gitmo on the Platte" (the holding center for protestors arrested during the DNC) and the interviews he conducted with fellow detainees.

The Downtown Denver police sweep, the only of its kind during the DNC, became the modus operandi at the RNC where police raided the home rented by I-witness video (without a valid warrant) and made mass arrests, lumping journalists and demonstrators together into paddy wagons and charging forty "credentialed" journalists with interference and trespassing. Amy Goodman was part of one such mass arrest. As she proclaimed her status as "press" in the police wagon, another woman asked her, "What makes you more special than us?" Goodman argued that when "the press" is detained, democracy is detained ("Amy Goodman . . . " 2008). Her response, while accurate in a symbolic sense, does not take into account the increasingly blurred line between the press and the public—literally the citizen journalists that populated both conventions.

What kinds of writing skills were necessary in that situation? Chadwick's students and my students were supposed to learn how to document an event— what they also learned was how the ground can quickly shift from public (where one's first and fourth amendment rights are protected) to private (with charges of trespassing) and how people do manage to create public voices on public issues despite severe opposition. When Lafer and his colleagues pressed employers about what job skills college students needed so desperately in order to make America competitive again, they replied with what they call "unobserved skill": interaction, ability to fit in, friendliness, cooperation, and ability to smile and show up on time. The truth is "the demand for both education and occupational skills grew most in the 1960s, tapered off in the 1970s, and slowed further during the 1980s and 1990s" (Lafer 2004, 67). While those "unobserved skills" are probably a factor in employment (and many of us reinforce these skills in the class—other than the ability to smile, maybe), they do not account for the

> driving economic trends nor to they guarantee upward mobility. Incomes and jobs and, as Chadwick's student and my students discovered, public voice and political influence "are shaped more powerfully by factors completely unrelated to skill" (Lafer 2004, 67).

So what? So we have gotten ourselves here, and so . . . so what? Are we expecting an ending? The wrap-up with a beautiful bow? Is that the genre expectation? Do we close on a "bummer" note or do we offer "hope" (echoing our new, centrist president)? Perhaps this place is the place where the fire burns, where we disappear in a puff of smoke, where we morph into something else . . . but what? How do we change the discourse, construct new possibilities, new ways of being? Because we are language users, we make our worlds every day. We have room to move, to be, to live, to teach, to learn, to enact. To breathe.

AFTERWORD

Shortly before *Composing Public Space* arrived in the mail, my sister sent me two local news items about her daughter's high school. My sister and niece, along with the rest of my family, live in a central Ohio town, Marysville, that has seemed to me a canary in the coalmine for economic and social miseries soon spreading everywhere. In the late 1970s, as U.S. auto manufacturers shut down plants across the upper Midwest, Marysville became home to one of central Ohio's three nonunion Honda plants. "Payday loan" and pawn shops moved into the dying downtown, since a nonunion paycheck stretches just so far, and temporary employment agencies sprang up, since thousands of Honda's employees—the corporation has been unwilling to disclose how many—are classified as "temporary." With the 1990s came the housing developments, their appealingly bucolic names reminiscent of the farmland they'd replaced and their even more appealing "balloon mortgage" terms eagerly sought by families like my sister's who, after migrating to Marysville following layoffs in three other states, had been camping in my mother's semifinished basement. By late 2008 my sister's (now ex-) husband was in the last months of employment by a company specializing in packing up manufacturing plants to be shipped south—not only to Mexico but to Alabama and Arkansas. Their house, like thousands in the region, went into foreclosure, central Ohio's foreclosure rate outpacing the rest of the state. The unemployment rate reached toward 10 percent, nearly on par with the northern "Rust Belt" counties abandoned by U.S. auto and steel in the last major slump. Meanwhile, newspaper headlines celebrated the apparent fact that in the midst of global economic freefall, Honda had not laid off a single employee. Only a few of those news stories noted, in passing, that Honda had dropped its temp workers. Marysville's temp agencies have vanished. The payday loan and pawn shops remain.

The latest news reports my sister sent me were not about layoffs, fore-closures, and other symptoms of deepening economic malaise—or not directly. Headlined "Racism Problem at Marysville High School?" and "Student Tattoo Violates Dress Code, Students Punished," they reported on the racial harassment and threats suffered by one of the town's few African American families. The latest incident involved a white male stu-dent who verbally abused the family's teenage daughter in a high-school hallway between classes, then lifted his shirt to reveal a red swastika tat-tooed to his chest. With the links to these reports, on the websites of two Columbus television news programs, my sister noted that she could not wait for my niece to graduate so they could finally clear out.

But in fact, that teenage boy's racism isn't homegrown—something my sister and niece can escape by leaving this particular town behind. In the same week I received these news items from my sister, Black students at the University of California San Diego were on the march following a series of racist attacks, including a noose hung in the school's library. This racism is fed by corporate-media millionaires like Fox News' Glenn Beck who urges viewers to "take back our country," Tea Partiers—primarily middle-class and college educated, according to recent CNN and *New York Times* reports (CNN Opinion Research 2010; Zernike and Thee-Brenan 2010)—forcing African American and gay congressmen to run their gauntlet of vile abuse, and politicians like Arizona Governor Jan Brewer who, as I write, has signed a law legitimating racial profiling—and along with it the notion that immigrants (or African Americans or women) are stealing American (or whites' or men's) jobs and undermin-ing "our" way of life. It's not that the Becks, Brewers, and Birthers repre-sent a majority of the U.S. population or confirm that we are a "center-right" nation. It is the case, however, that they've tapped into a deep well of genuine economic anxiety and legitimate economic anger—injecting into that anxiety and anger their racist, xenophobic, homophobic, and antigovernment toxins. Very far from a private or individual matter—the problem of a teenage boy who wasn't "raised right" or a small Ohio town that's hopelessly "backward"—racism is public, pervasive, and in this po-litical moment deliberately deployed to defund the public programs and derail social reforms desperately needed by those for whom right-wing populists claim to speak.

And yet, even as the headline of one news item sent by my sister—"Racism Problem at Marysville High School?"—points toward potential discussion through which conditions (including the economic conditions I sketched at this piece's start) breeding such toxicity might be examined, the articles themselves steer away not only from racism as a thoroughly social issue but as being the central issue at all.

Consider: The first article starts with five one- and two-sentence paragraphs in which we learn that the African American student accosted in the hallway has been, not once but many times, threatened with being hung from a tree, called a "silver-backed monkey," and advised with her family to "go back to Africa" and not "spread their diseases here . . . in Ohio" ("Racism" 2010). Then comes the turn as we're told that this student also "admitted" to using "foul language" in speaking back to her attacker and that, according to school officials, she had also used "racial slurs" against him ("Racism" 2010). The article concludes with the school superintendent stating that while "other African-American families have complained," he "doesn't believe there is a racial problem at the high school," his assertion followed by a rejoinder from the girl's mother: "Walk a mile in my shoes. . . . Let someone walk up to you and threaten to hang you from a tree, call you a (racial slur) and see how you feel" ("Racism" 2010).

The second report does not even gesture toward differentiating between the white student's verbal attack and the Black student's defensive response; relying on a single source, the superintendent, this article does not attempt to "balance" the school's assertion that racism is not a problem with the family's insistence that it is. Instead this article opens with the statement that "racial slurs exchanged between students were grounds enough for punishment" ("Student Tattoo" 2010). The white student, we learn, was suspended because his tattoo violates the school's dress code, or more specifically, because bringing the tattoo out from under wraps violates the school's dress code: "If it's covered," the superintendent explained, "as it was normally, that's an issue between that family" ("Student Tattoo" 2010). *Also* found to be in violation of the school's conduct code and so suspended for *her* use of "foul language" was the victim. Indeed, the other article reports that this is the second or third time she has been suspended for arguing back when "all kinds of things" were said to her ("Racism" 2010). The second article, maintaining a tight focus on how both students had violated school codes, concludes with the superintendent declaring, "Bottom line, inappropriate. . . . It's not going to be tolerated, it's really that simple" ("Student Tattoo" 2010). What is "it" that is "not going to be tolerated"? Not swastikas per se, which remain permissible, a private family matter so long as they stay, as they "normally" do, out of sight. Not racism either, which is set aside with the article's opening premise that both students had created together the grounds for their punishment. Instead, throughout this article the central issue, the public problem is not racism, is not resurgent white supremacy but is instead individual conduct.

The dearth of opportunities for African American families in this school district to "self-represent"; the superintendent's liberal guardianship of high-school hallway "neutrality" where neither racist expression nor vocal defense against racism will be tolerated; the news reports' containment and dismissal of a public controversy: Here we have a textbook case of a social issue's privatization. The first article takes an *eventful* situation, a *developing* story and contains it with the détente of "he said" versus "she said." The second article forecloses eventfulness, the shock of the swastika, altogether by asserting, from first sentence to last, that this isn't really even a *news* story to be reported on in the public interest. Rather, it is a case of violated behavior codes, easily dealt with through a mundane punishment that schools regularly mete out to individual students.

The news reports' neutralizing and privatizing moves are, of course, no surprise. The hallmark of what French linguist François-René Huyghe (1991) calls "la langue de cotton"—the wooly, obfuscating, stupefying language of neoliberalism—is an already decided upon consensus in a rhetorical universe that takes equality as a given, denying any existence of dramatic power imbalances and inequities. Hence the first article presents the superintendent's view and the mother's as if both this professional-class white man and this working-class Black woman exist on a plane of perfect equality, as if readers are simply free to choose which view to accept, no consequences either way. And hence the second article begins with the assumption that all is already settled: both students are guilty, both will be punished.

What is also no surprise—and what *Composing Public Space* works to illuminate and disturb—is the school superintendent's seemingly commonsensical response, taking the substantive question of racism in the town's schools and neutralizing it as a procedural issue of student conduct—their dress, their word choices—on school grounds. Though I'd like to say I would have responded differently, here I recall a recent MLA panel and how, when a prominent literary critic denounced compositionists for using their "power" to "impose" their "political agendas" on students instead of "sticking" to "skills," the other panelists and I retreated into claims of neutral facilitation and rhetorical formalism. *No bias, no agenda, no politics and messy social engagement in our classrooms. No, we teach students to examine arguments, to read against the grain of sources, to substantiate claims*—as if Aristotle, and not the movements for Black and Chicano power, for third world and women's liberation, is the progenitor of critical pedagogy. Fact is, more than three decades of assault on every form of collective action and public advocacy have taken their toll. We have all learned the privatized habits of (even the liberal) mind that have played handmaid to the material erosion of public space, voice, and entitlements.

We are also just at the very start of witnessing the consequences of the shrinking of public space, the erosion of the very idea of public education, and the Left's disavowal of a pedagogical agenda even as free marketeers and social conservatives step up their aggressive literacy sponsorship. Texas Board of Education members, none of whom are historians, vote in a new curricula "stressing the superiority of American capitalism, questioning the Founding Fathers' commitment to a purely secular government and presenting Republican political philosophies in a more positive light" (McKinley 2010). With its draconian anti-immigrant law, Arizona's legislature also passes a ban on funding any school program that would "[p]romote resentment of a particular race or class of people," "[a] dvocate ethnic solidarity instead of the treatment of pupils as individuals," or is "designed primarily for students of a particular ethnic group" (Arizona 2010). From Washington, Education Secretary Arne Duncan urges cash-strapped states to make their public schools eligible for a share of $4.3 billion in federal assistance—by breaking key provisions of teachers' union contracts and turning at least 10 percent of a state's schools over to charter-school operators (U.S. Department of Education 2010). In Ohio, the Department of Education responds to a first wave of multimillion-dollar cuts to public school budgets by announcing its new "partnership" with the U.S. Army, contracted to help with math and physics teaching in middle and high schools through its first-person-shooter video game "America's Army" (America's Army Team 2008; see also Welch 2008). And in Marysville, news cameras again descend when a small but vocal group of parents seek a blanket ban on clips from films with a rating other than "G" being shown in any high school class (Zachariah 2010).

The past months have also seen people—many for the very first time, having never before thought of themselves as "activists"—starting to rally: mass actions for LGBT rights and against the slashing and burning of public education, protests against resurgent racism and for immigrant rights. Public space, voice, and rights are not being ceded without a struggle. In Marysville, my sister launched an anticensorship group, succeeding in lifting the ban on classroom films (although the compromise brokered by the superintendent includes a multipage procedure teachers must follow before showing a clip from a film with a "PG-13" or "R" rating).

What *Composing Public Space* reminds us is that our teaching in this moment cannot be neutral and that as educators and writing teachers we need to relearn the fullest language, the fullest rhetorical strategies to reclaim, hang onto, and expand the public space, public issues, public resources lost to privatization's long reign. Have we, for instance, become simply accustomed to advising our students that mediation and bridge building are always preferable to agonistic confrontation? Do we piously teach the "rhetoric of the open hand" as superior to that of the "closed fist"? If the answer—as I think it is for many in our field—is yes, we should read again the conclusion to Edward P. J. Corbett's famous 1969 essay:

> The open hand and the closed fist have the same basic skeletal structure. If rhetoric is, as Aristotle defined it, "a discovery of all the available means of persuasion," let us be prepared to open and close that hand as the occasion demands. (296)

In 1969 mass public action, accompanied by every variation of the resolute fist of resistance—from the Chicano Power, Black Power and American Indian Movement to the burgeoning movements for Women's and Gay Liberation—was resulting in a profound and consequential opening up of public space, education and curricula that today, decades of rollback later, I have to convince my students really did happen, really was—and is—possible. Today we should also recall that there were teachers with students who walked out and sat in. Imagine that—what the authors of *Composing Public Space* are challenging us to do—think of a world in which teachers were not neutral and objective, a world in which we not only teach the forms of argument but engage, take on, the biggest arguments of our time.

—*Nancy Welch*

Works Cited

America's Army Team. 2008. "New Army Game Applications Look to Boost Tech Interests." Army News Service, 19 September. www.army.mil/-news/2008/09/19/12589-new-army-game-applications-look-to-boost-tech-interests/.

Arizona House of Representatives. 2010. HB 2281. "Prohibited Courses, Discipline [sic], Schools" www.azleg.gov/FormatDocument.asp?inDoc=/legtext/49leg/2r/summary/h.hb2281_03-18-10_houseengrossed.doc.htm.

CNN Opinion Research Poll. 2010. 12–15 February. http://i2.cdn.turner.com/cnn/2010/images/02/17/rel4b.pdf.

Corbett, Edward P. J. 1969. "The Rhetoric of the Open Hand and the Rhetoric of the Closed Fist." *College Composition and Communication* 5: 288–96.

Huyghe, François-René. 1991. *La Langue de Cotton*. Paris: Laffront.

McKinley, James Jr. 2010. "Texas Conservatives Win Curriculum Change." *New York Times* 12 March, A10.

"Racism Problem at Marysville High School?" 2010. 26 February. www2.nbc4i.com/news/2010/feb/26/marysville_schoolracism-ar-23639/.

"Student Tattoo Violates Dress Code, Students Punished." 2010. 26 February. www.10tv.com/live/content/local/stories/2010/02/26/story-marysville-students-disciplined-tattoo.html?type=rss&cat=&sid=102.

U.S. Department of Education. 2010. "Race to the Top Program Guidance and Frequently Asked Questions." 13 January. www2.ed.gov/programs/racetothetop/faq.pdf.

Welch, Nancy. 2008. "'This Video Game We Call War': Multimodal Recruitment in America's Army Game." *Reflections: A Journal of Writing, Community Literacy, and Service Learning*. Winter. 162–91.

Zachariah, Holly. 2010. "Marysville Schools Revise Movie Policy." 16 March. *Dispatch Politics*. www.dispatchpolitics.com/live/content/local_news/stories/2010/03/16/copy/marysville-revises-movie-policy.html?sid=101.

Zernike, Kate, and Megan Thee-Brenan. 2010. "Poll Finds Tea Party Backers Wealthier and More Educated." *New York Times* 14 April, A1.

BIBLIOGRAPHY

Abel, Jessica, and Ira Glass. 1999. *Radio: An Illustrated Guide*. Chicago: WBEZ Alliance Inc.

Allison, Jay. 2001. "Storytelling on the Radio Builds Community, On-Air and Off." *Transom Review* 1.11 (2001): 15 Feb. www.transom.org/guests/review/200110.review.jallison.html (accessed February 15, 2008).

"Amy Goodman Arrested at RNC." 2008. *YouTube*. www.youtube.com/watch?v=oYjyvkR0bGQ (accessed September 1, 2008).

Aronowitz, Stanley, and Henry A. Giroux. 1987. *Education Under Seige*. New York: Routledge.

Badiou, Alain. 2006. *Briefings on Existence: A Short Treatise on Transitory Ontology*. Trans. Norman Madrasz. Albany, NY: State University of New York Press.

Barthes, Roland. 1977. "The Death of the Author." *Image-Music-Text*. Trans. Stephen Heath. London: Fontana.

Bartholomae, David. 2007. "Inventing the University." *The St. Martin's Guide to Teaching Writing*, 382–96. Eds. Cheryl Glenn and Melissa Goldthwaite. 6th ed. New York: Macmillan.

Berthoff, Ann E. 1978. *Forming/Thinking Writing: The Composing Imagination*. Rochelle Park, NJ: Hayden.

Bérubé, Michael. 2006. *What's Liberal About the Liberal Arts?: Classroom Politics and "Bias" in Higher Education*. New York: W.W. Norton.

Bleich, David. 2001. "The Materiality of Language and the Pedagogy of Exchange." *Pedagogy* 1: 117–41.

Brannon, Lil, Jennifer Poole Courtney, Cynthia Urbanski, Shane Woodward, Jeanie Reynolds, Anthony Iannone, Karen Haag, Karen Mach, Lacy Manship, and Mary Kendrick. 2008. "The Five-Paragraph Essay and the Deficit Model of Education." *English Journal* 92:2: 16–21.

Brown, Judy. 2003. "Fire." *Teaching with Fire: Poetry That Sustains the Courage to Teach*. San Francisco: Jossey-Bass.

Campbell, Bebe Moore. 1989. *Sweet Summer: Growing Up With and Without My Dad*. New York: Putnam.

Carroll, Vincent. 2006. "Molding the Future." *The Rocky Mountain News*. 9 March: 38A.

CBS/AP. 2006. "Teacher Probed over Bush Remarks." *CBS Evening News*. 3 March. www.cbsnews.com/stories/2006/03/03/politics/main1364883 .shtml (accessed September 10, 2007).

Chasseguet-Smirgel, Janine. 1984. *Creativity and Perversion*. New York: W.W. Norton.

Cisneros, Sandra. 2002. *Caramelo, or, Puro Cuento: A Novel*. New York: Knopf.

Cixous, Hélène. 2001. "The Laugh of the Medusa." *The Rhetorical Tradition: Readings from Classical Times to the Present*, 1524–36. 2nd ed. Eds. Patricia Bizzell and Bruce Herzberg. New York: Bedford/St. Martin's.

Clavreul, Jean. 1980. "The Perverse Couple." *Returning to Freud: Clinical Psychoanalysis in the School of Lacan*, 215–33. Ed and trans. Stuart Schneiderman. New Haven: Yale University Press.

Clifford, John. 1991. "The Subject Is Discourse." *Contending with Words: Composition and Rhetoric in a Postmodern Age*, 31–51. Ed. Patricia Harkin and John Schilb. New York: Modern Language Association.

"Colorado Woman Wins Grueling Arctic Race." 2008. *Colorado Matters*. CPR, Denver. 8 March.

Comstock, Michelle. 2004. "Writing Vicariously: The Politics of Presence in the Distance Learning Classroom." *Current* 8. www.cwrl.utexas.edu/ currents/fall04/comstock.html (accessed September 14, 2009).

Cooper, Marilyn. 2007. "Labor Practices and the Use Value of Technologies." *Labor, Writing Technologies, and the Shaping of Composition in the Academy*, 213–28. Eds. Pamela Takayoshi and Patricia Sullivan. Cresskill, NJ: Hampton Press.

de Certeau, Michel. 1984. *The Practice of Everyday Life*. Trans. Steven Rendall. Berkeley: University of California Press.

Dillon, Sam. 2005. "At Public Universities, Warnings of Privatization." *New York Times* 16 Oct: 12.

Diversity Data. 2000. "Mobile, AL: Summary Profile." *Harvard School of Public Health*. http://diversitydata.sph.harvard.edu/Data/Profiles/Show .aspx?loc=837 (accessed September 14, 2009).

Durlin, Martin, and Cathy Melio. 2006. "The Grassroots Radio Movement in the U.S." 26 Nov. *Grassroots Radio Coalition*. www.grradio.org/about. html (accessed August 2, 2007).

Elbow, Peter. 1973. *Writing Without Teachers*. New York: Oxford University Press.

Fairclough, Norman. 2003. *Analyzing Discourse: Textual Analysis for Social Research*. New York: Routledge.

Fanon, Frantz. 1996. "Images, Words, and Narrative Epistemology." *College English* 58: 914–33.

———. 1982. *Black Skin, White Masks*. Trans. Charles Lam Markmann. New York: Grove Press.

Fleckenstein, Kristie S. 2003. *Embodied Literacies: Imageword and a Poetics of Teaching*. Carbondale, IL: Southern Illinois University Press.

———. 1996. "Images, Words, and Narrative Epistemology." *College English* 58 (8): 914–33.

Fox News. 2003. "Teacher's Anti-Bush Pin Stirs Controversy." 10 March. www .foxnews.com/story/0,2933,80226,00.html (accessed September 10, 2007).

Freire, Paulo. 1995. *Pedagogy of the Oppressed*. Trans. Myra Bergman Ramos. New York: Continuum.

Freud, Sigmund. 1997. *Sexuality and the Psychology of Love*. New York: Simon & Schuster.

Gasper, Phil. 2009. "Marxism and Religion." *International Socialist Review* 63.1: 13–14.

Gertzenzang, James. 2003. "The Right Man: The Surprise Presidency of George W. Bush." *The Journal Gazette* 7 Jan.

Gorzelsky, Gwen. 2003. "Making Contact: Experience, Representation, and Difference." *JAC* 23: 397–427.

Grossberg, Lawrence. 1992. *We Gotta Get Out of This Place: Popular Conservatism and Postmodern Culture*. New York: Routledge.

Hawisher, Gail E., and Patricia A. Sullivan. 1999. "Fleeting Images: Women Visually Writing the Web." *Passions, Pedagogies, and 21st Century Technologies*, 268–91. Eds. Gail E. Hawisher and Cynthia L. Selfe. Logan, UT: Utah State University Press.

Heath, Shirley Brice. 1983. *Ways with Words: Language, Life, and Work in Communities and Classrooms*. New York: Cambridge University Press.

Holland, Dorothy, Debra Skinner, William Lachiotte, Jr., and Carole Cain. 1998. *Identity and Agency in Cultural Worlds*. Cambridge, MA: Harvard University Press.

hooks, bell. 1996. "Choosing the Margin as a Space of Radical Openness." *Women, Knowledge, and Reality: Explorations in Feminist Philosophy*, 48–55. Eds. Ann Garry and Marilyn Pearsall. 2nd ed. New York: Routledge.

Horner, Bruce. 1999. "Rethinking the 'Sociality' of Error." *Representing the "Other": Basic Writers and the Teaching of Basic Writing*, 139–65. Eds. Bruce Horner and Min-Zhan Lu. Urbana, IL: NCTE.

In-Seo, Byung. 2007. "Speaking My Mind: Defending the Five-Paragraph Essay." *English Journal* 97.2: 15–16.

Jarratt, Susan C. 1998. "Introductions: As We Were Saying…." *Feminism and Composition Studies: In Other Words*, 1–18. Eds. Susan C. Jarratt and Lynn Worsham. New York: Modern Language Association of America.

King, Martin J. 2007. "Controlling the Right to Protest." *FBI Law Enforcement Bulletin* 76.5. www.fbi.gov/publications/leb/2007/may2007/may2007leb.htm#page20 (accessed August 24, 2008).

Kohl, Herbert. 1994. *"I Won't Learn from You": And Other Thoughts on Creative Maladjustment.* New York: New Press.

Lafer, Gordon. 2004. *The Job Training Charade.* Ithaca, NY: Cornell University Press.

Lake Research Partners. 2006. "Key Findings from a Recent Nationwide Survey of Voters," 16 July. Pro-Choice America. www.prochoiceamerica.org/elections/2006/Election-Poll-Summary.pdf (accessed September 10, 2006.

Latour, Bruno. 2005. "From Realpolitik to Dingpolitik or How to Make Things Public." *Making Things Public: Atmospheres of Democracy,* 14–43. Eds. Bruno Latour and Peter Weibel. Cambridge, MA: MIT Press.

Livesey, Margot. 1994. "How to Tell a True Story." *The Best Writing on Writing,* 72–84. Ed. Jack Heffron. Cincinnati, OH: Story Press.

Lu, Min-Zhan. 1999. "The Vitality of the Ungrateful Receiver: Making Giving Mutual Between Composition and Postcolonial Studies." *JAC: A Journal of Composition Theory* 19: 335–58.

Martinez, Elizabeth, and Arnoldo Garcia. 2000. "What Is 'Neo-Liberalism'?" *Global Economy 101.* 26 Feb. Global Exchange. www.globalexchange.org/campaigns/econ101/neoliberalDefined.html (accessed October 10, 2003).

Marx, Karl. 1976. *Capital: Volume 1: A Critique of Political Economy.* New York: Penguin.

McWilliam, Erica. 1997. "Beyond the Missionary Position: Teacher Desire and Radical Pedagogy." *Learning Desire: Perspectives on Pedagogy, Culture, and the Unsaid,* 217–36. Ed. Sharon Todd. New York: Routledge.

Miller, Richard E. 1998. "The Arts of Complicity: Pragmatism and the Culture of Schooling." *College English* 61: 10–28.

Mitchell, Don. 2003. *The Right to the City: Social Justice and the Fight for Public Space.* New York: Guilford Press.

Mullen, Mark. 2006. "Colorado Classroom Controversy Stirs Debate." *Today.* 7 March. www.msnbc.msn.com/id/11709270 (accessed September 10, 2007).

Onwuachi-Willig, Angela. 2005. "Just Another Brother on the SCT?: What Justice Clarence Thomas Teaches Us About the Influence of Racial Identity." *Iowa Law Review* 90: 931–1010.

Ratcliffe, Krista. 2005. *Rhetorical Listening: Identification, Gender, Whiteness.* Carbondale, IL: Southern Illinois University Press.

Reynolds, Nedra. 1998. "Composition's Imagined Geographies: The Politics of Space in the Frontier, City, and Cyberspace." *College Composition and Communication* 50: 12–35.

Roberts-Miller, Patricia. 2004. *Deliberate Conflict: Argument, Political Theory, and Composition Classes.* Carbondale, IL: Southern Illinois University Press.

Rodriguez, Luis J. 2005. *Always Running: La Vida Loca, Gang Days in L.A.* New York: Simon & Schuster.

Rose, Mike. 1989. *Lives on the Boundary: The Struggles and Achievements of America's Underprepared.* New York: Free Press.

Roy, Arundhati. 2001. *Power Politics.* Cambridge, MA: South End Press.

Schafer, R. Murray. 1994. *The Soundscape: Our Sonic Environment and the Tuning of the World.* Rochester, VT: Destiny.

Schultz, David. 2005. "The Corporate University in American Society." *Logos* 4.4: *www.logosjournal.com/issue_4.4/schultz.htm* (accessed September 7, 2006).

Shlain, Leonard. 1998. *The Alphabet Versus the Goddess: The Conflict Between Word and Image.* New York: Viking.

Shor, Ira. 1987. *Critical Teaching and Everyday Life.* Chicago: The University of Chicago Press.

Slater, Lauren. 2000. *Lying: A Metaphorical Memoir.* New York: Random House.

Soja, Edward W. 1996. *Thirdspace: Journeys to Los Angeles and Other Real-and-Imagined Places.* Cambridge, MA: Blackwell.

Sondergard, Sidney. 2002. *Sharpening Her Pen: Strategies of Rhetorical Violence by Early Modern English Women Writers.* Selinsgrove, PA: Susquehanna University Press.

Stuckey, Elspeth. 1991. *The Violence of Literacy.* Portsmouth, NH: Boynton/Cook Publishers.

Takayoshi, Pamela, and Patricia Sullivan. 2007. "Introduction: Literacy Work in a Technology-Rich Culture: Issues at the Intersection of Labor, Technology, and Writing Instruction." *Labor, Writing Technologies, and the Shaping of Composition in the Academy*, 1–22. Eds. Pamela Takayoshi and Patricia Sullivan. Cresskill, NJ: Hampton Press.

Tannen, Deborah. 1991. *You Just Don't Understand: Women and Men in Conversation.* New York: Ballantine Books.

Therese, Marie. 2006. "Teacher Jay Bennish Fights Back—Goes to NBC, Not FOX." 8 March. *News Hound.* www.newshounds.us/2006/03/08/teacher_jay_bennish_fights_back_goes_to_nbc_not_fox.php (accessed September 10, 2007).

Tuana, Nancy. 1994. *Feminist Interpretations of Plato.* University Park, PA: Penn State University Press.

University of South Alabama. 2001. "Self-Study Report." Fall. *University of South Alabama Office of Academic Affairs.* http://74.125.113.132/search?q=ca che:ZU5Vk6XbutUJ:www.southalabama.edu/academicaffairs/ INTRODUCTION,%2520Self-Study.doc+2000+university+of+sou th+alabama+student+data&cd=1&hl=en&ct=clnk&gl=us (accessed September 14, 2009).

Vidali, Amy. 2007. "Texts of Our Institutional Lives: Performing the Rhetorical Freak Show: Disability, Student Writing, and College Admissions." *College English* 69: 615–41.

Villanueva, Victor. 2002. "On Syllabi." *Strategies for Teaching First-Year Composition*, 98–101. Ed. Duane Roen. Urbana, IL: NCTE.

Welch, Nancy. 2008. *Living Room: Teaching Public Writing in a Privatized World.* Portsmouth, NH: Boynton/Cook Publishers.

———. 2004. "Privat(ized) Writing: The Struggle for Rhetorical Space in a Post-Publicity Era." College Composition and Communication Conference. San Antonio Hyatt, San Antonio, TX. 25 March.

———. 1997. *Getting Restless: Rethinking Revision in Writing Instruction.* Portsmouth, NH: Boynton/Cook Publishers.

Williams, Walter. 2006. "Indoctrination of Our Youth." 22 Feb. *Capitalism Magazine.* www.capmag.com/article.asp?ID=4579 (accessed September 10, 2007).

Winnicott, Donald. 1963. "Transitional Objects and Transitional Phenomena." *International Journal of Psychoanalysis* 34: 89–97.

Wojnarowicz, David. 1991. *Close to the Knives: A Memoir of Disintegration.* New York: Vintage Books.

Yagelski, Robert. 2006. "'Radical to Many in the Educational Community': The Process Movement After the Hurricanes." Review essay. *College English* 68 (May): 531–44.